STUDY SECRETS COURSE!

Dear Customer,

Struggle with tests? Short on time? Not sure where to even start studying? We have partnered with Mometrix to offer you their Study Secrets Course. Mometrix designed the course to help every student, no matter what study scenario you are in.

This online course guides you through the full process, from study preparation to test day, so you'll be ready to ace your next exam. The Study Secrets Course contains **14 in-depth lessons** that break down top study strategies, **15+ video reviews** that walk you step by step through each topic, and **5 downloadable resources** to help you apply the strategies.

Online Study Secrets Course

Course Features:

- Techniques to Conquer Procrastination
- Steps to Building a Study Plan
- 7 Effective Note-Taking Methods
- Test-Taking Tips
- Memory Techniques and Mnemonics
- 50 Quick and Unusual Study Tips
- How to Create SMART Goals
- How to Study Math
- And much more!

Everyone learns differently, so they have tailored their Study Secrets Course to ensure every learner has what they need to prepare for their upcoming exam or semester.

To purchase this course and start studying, visit them at mometrix.com/university/studysecrets or simply scan this QR code with your smartphone.

If you have any questions or concerns, please contact them at support@mometrix.com.

Sincerely,

Online Resources & Audiobook Access

Included with your purchase are multiple online resources. This includes all three practice tests in interactive format and this study guide in audiobook format. We also have a convenient study timer to help you manage your time.

Instructions for accessing these resources can be found on the last page of this book.

CJBAT Study Guide Florida 2025 and 2026

3 Practice Exams and CJBAT Test Prep Book for Law Enforcement and Correctional Officers [3rd Edition]

Lydia Morrison

Copyright © 2025 by TPB Publishing

All rights reserved. No part of this publication may be reproduced, distributed, or transmitted in any form or by any means, including photocopying, recording, or other electronic or mechanical methods, without the prior written permission of the publisher, except in the case of brief quotations embodied in critical reviews and certain other noncommercial uses permitted by copyright law.

Written and edited by TPB Publishing.

TPB Publishing is not associated with or endorsed by any official testing organization. TPB Publishing is a publisher of unofficial educational products. All test and organization names are trademarks of their respective owners. Content in this book is included for utilitarian purposes only and does not constitute an endorsement by TPB Publishing of any particular point of view.

Interested in buying more than 10 copies of our product? Contact us about bulk discounts:
bulkorders@studyguideteam.com

ISBN 13: 9781637752159

Table of Contents

Welcome *2*

Quick Overview *3*

Test-Taking Strategies *4*

Introduction to the CJBAT *8*

Study Prep Plan for the CJBAT *10*

Written Comprehension *11*

   Literary Analysis 11

   Main Ideas and Supporting Details 15

   Inferences in a Text 19

   Author's Use of Language 22

   Practice Quiz 28

   Answer Explanations 30

Written Expression *31*

   Spelling 31

   Clarity 37

   Vocabulary 46

   Practice Quiz 54

   Answer Explanations 55

Memorization *56*

   Practice Image 61

   Answers 63

Reasoning *64*

   Practice Quiz 71

Answer Explanations 73

Personal Characteristics/Behavioral Attributes 74
Practice Quiz 81
Answer Explanations 82

Practice Test #1 83
Memorization 83
Written Comprehension 92
Written Expression 98
Reasoning 99

Answer Explanations #1 105
Memorization 105
Written Comprehension 106
Written Expression 109
Reasoning 110

Practice Test #2 113
Memorization 113
Written Comprehension 116
Written Expression 121
Reasoning 122

Answer Explanations #2 128
Memorization 128
Written Comprehension 128
Written Expression 129
Reasoning 130

Practice Test #3 133

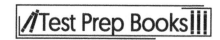

Memorization 133
Written Comprehension 136
Written Expression 140
Reasoning 142

Answer Explanations #3 .... *147*

Memorization 147
Written Comprehension 147
Written Expression 148
Reasoning 149

Online Resources & Audiobook Access *153*

Welcome

Dear Reader,

Welcome to your new Test Prep Books study guide! We are pleased that you chose us to help you prepare for your exam. There are many study options to choose from, and we appreciate you choosing us. Studying can be a daunting task, but we have designed a smart, effective study guide to help prepare you for what lies ahead.

Whether you're a parent helping your child learn and grow, a high school student working hard to get into your dream college, or a nursing student studying for a complex exam, we want to help give you the tools you need to succeed. We hope this study guide gives you the skills and the confidence to thrive, and we can't thank you enough for allowing us to be part of your journey.

In an effort to continue to improve our products, we welcome feedback from our customers. We look forward to hearing from you. Suggestions, success stories, and criticisms can all be communicated by emailing us at info@studyguideteam.com.

Sincerely,
Test Prep Books Team

Quick Overview

As you draw closer to taking your exam, effective preparation becomes more and more important. Thankfully, you have this study guide to help you get ready. Use this guide to help keep your studying on track and refer to it often.

This study guide contains several key sections that will help you be successful on your exam. The guide contains tips for what you should do the night before and the day of the test. Also included are test-taking tips. Knowing the right information is not always enough. Many well-prepared test takers struggle with exams. These tips will help equip you to accurately read, assess, and answer test questions.

A large part of the guide is devoted to showing you what content to expect on the exam and to helping you better understand that content. In this guide are practice test questions so that you can see how well you have grasped the content. Then, answer explanations are provided so that you can understand why you missed certain questions.

Don't try to cram the night before you take your exam. This is not a wise strategy for a few reasons. First, your retention of the information will be low. Your time would be better used by reviewing information you already know rather than trying to learn a lot of new information. Second, you will likely become stressed as you try to gain a large amount of knowledge in a short amount of time. Third, you will be depriving yourself of sleep. So be sure to go to bed at a reasonable time the night before. Being well-rested helps you focus and remain calm.

Be sure to eat a substantial breakfast the morning of the exam. If you are taking the exam in the afternoon, be sure to have a good lunch as well. Being hungry is distracting and can make it difficult to focus. You have hopefully spent lots of time preparing for the exam. Don't let an empty stomach get in the way of success!

When traveling to the testing center, leave earlier than needed. That way, you have a buffer in case you experience any delays. This will help you remain calm and will keep you from missing your appointment time at the testing center.

Be sure to pace yourself during the exam. Don't try to rush through the exam. There is no need to risk performing poorly on the exam just so you can leave the testing center early. Allow yourself to use all of the allotted time if needed.

Remain positive while taking the exam even if you feel like you are performing poorly. Thinking about the content you should have mastered will not help you perform better on the exam.

Once the exam is complete, take some time to relax. Even if you feel that you need to take the exam again, you will be well served by some down time before you begin studying again. It's often easier to convince yourself to study if you know that it will come with a reward!

Test-Taking Strategies

1. Predicting the Answer

When you feel confident in your preparation for a multiple-choice test, try predicting the answer before reading the answer choices. This is especially useful on questions that test objective factual knowledge. By predicting the answer before reading the available choices, you eliminate the possibility that you will be distracted or led astray by an incorrect answer choice. You will feel more confident in your selection if you read the question, predict the answer, and then find your prediction among the answer choices. After using this strategy, be sure to still read all of the answer choices carefully and completely. If you feel unprepared, you should not attempt to predict the answers. This would be a waste of time and an opportunity for your mind to wander in the wrong direction.

2. Reading the Whole Question

Too often, test takers scan a multiple-choice question, recognize a few familiar words, and immediately jump to the answer choices. Test authors are aware of this common impatience, and they will sometimes prey upon it. For instance, a test author might subtly turn the question into a negative, or he or she might redirect the focus of the question right at the end. The only way to avoid falling into these traps is to read the entirety of the question carefully before reading the answer choices.

3. Looking for Wrong Answers

Long and complicated multiple-choice questions can be intimidating. One way to simplify a difficult multiple-choice question is to eliminate all of the answer choices that are clearly wrong. In most sets of answers, there will be at least one selection that can be dismissed right away. If the test is administered on paper, the test taker could draw a line through it to indicate that it may be ignored; otherwise, the test taker will have to perform this operation mentally or on scratch paper. In either case, once the obviously incorrect answers have been eliminated, the remaining choices may be considered. Sometimes identifying the clearly wrong answers will give the test taker some information about the correct answer. For instance, if one of the remaining answer choices is a direct opposite of one of the eliminated answer choices, it may well be the correct answer. The opposite of obviously wrong is obviously right! Of course, this is not always the case. Some answers are obviously incorrect simply because they are irrelevant to the question being asked. Still, identifying and eliminating some incorrect answer choices is a good way to simplify a multiple-choice question.

4. Don't Overanalyze

Anxious test takers often overanalyze questions. When you are nervous, your brain will often run wild, causing you to make associations and discover clues that don't actually exist. If you feel that this may be a problem for you, do whatever you can to slow down during the test. Try taking a deep breath or counting to ten. As you read and consider the question, restrict yourself to the particular words used by the author. Avoid thought tangents about what the author *really* meant, or what he or she was *trying* to say. The only things that matter on a multiple-choice test are the words that are actually in the question. You must avoid reading too much into a multiple-choice question, or supposing that the writer meant something other than what he or she wrote.

Test-Taking Strategies

5. No Need for Panic

It is wise to learn as many strategies as possible before taking a multiple-choice test, but it is likely that you will come across a few questions for which you simply don't know the answer. In this situation, avoid panicking. Because most multiple-choice tests include dozens of questions, the relative value of a single wrong answer is small. As much as possible, you should compartmentalize each question on a multiple-choice test. In other words, you should not allow your feelings about one question to affect your success on the others. When you find a question that you either don't understand or don't know how to answer, just take a deep breath and do your best. Read the entire question slowly and carefully. Try rephrasing the question a couple of different ways. Then, read all of the answer choices carefully. After eliminating obviously wrong answers, make a selection and move on to the next question.

6. Confusing Answer Choices

When working on a difficult multiple-choice question, there may be a tendency to focus on the answer choices that are the easiest to understand. Many people, whether consciously or not, gravitate to the answer choices that require the least concentration, knowledge, and memory. This is a mistake. When you come across an answer choice that is confusing, you should give it extra attention. A question might be confusing because you do not know the subject matter to which it refers. If this is the case, don't

eliminate the answer before you have affirmatively settled on another. When you come across an answer choice of this type, set it aside as you look at the remaining choices. If you can confidently assert that one of the other choices is correct, you can leave the confusing answer aside. Otherwise, you will need to take a moment to try to better understand the confusing answer choice. Rephrasing is one way to tease out the sense of a confusing answer choice.

7. Your First Instinct

Many people struggle with multiple-choice tests because they overthink the questions. If you have studied sufficiently for the test, you should be prepared to trust your first instinct once you have carefully and completely read the question and all of the answer choices. There is a great deal of research suggesting that the mind can come to the correct conclusion very quickly once it has obtained all of the relevant information. At times, it may seem to you as if your intuition is working faster even than your reasoning mind. This may in fact be true. The knowledge you obtain while studying may be retrieved from your subconscious before you have a chance to work out the associations that support it. Verify your instinct by working out the reasons that it should be trusted.

8. Key Words

Many test takers struggle with multiple-choice questions because they have poor reading comprehension skills. Quickly reading and understanding a multiple-choice question requires a mixture of skill and experience. To help with this, try jotting down a few key words and phrases on a piece of scrap paper. Doing this concentrates the process of reading and forces the mind to weigh the relative importance of the question's parts. In selecting words and phrases to write down, the test taker thinks about the question more deeply and carefully. This is especially true for multiple-choice questions that are preceded by a long prompt.

9. Subtle Negatives

One of the oldest tricks in the multiple-choice test writer's book is to subtly reverse the meaning of a question with a word like *not* or *except*. If you are not paying attention to each word in the question, you can easily be led astray by this trick. For instance, a common question format is, "Which of the following is...?" Obviously, if the question instead is, "Which of the following is not...?," then the answer will be quite different. Even worse, the test makers are aware of the potential for this mistake and will include one answer choice that would be correct if the question were not negated or reversed. A test taker who misses the reversal will find what he or she believes to be a correct answer and will be so confident that he or she will fail to reread the question and discover the original error. The only way to avoid this is to practice a wide variety of multiple-choice questions and to pay close attention to each and every word.

10. Reading Every Answer Choice

It may seem obvious, but you should always read every one of the answer choices! Too many test takers fall into the habit of scanning the question and assuming that they understand the question because they recognize a few key words. From there, they pick the first answer choice that answers the question they believe they have read. Test takers who read all of the answer choices might discover that one of the latter answer choices is actually *more* correct. Moreover, reading all of the answer choices can remind you of facts related to the question that can help you arrive at the correct answer. Sometimes, a misstatement or incorrect detail in one of the latter answer choices will trigger your memory of the subject and will enable you to find the right answer. Failing to read all of the answer choices is like not reading all of the items on a restaurant menu: you might miss out on the perfect choice.

11. Spot the Hedges

One of the keys to success on multiple-choice tests is paying close attention to every word. This is never truer than with words like *almost*, *most*, *some*, and *sometimes*. These words are called "hedges" because they indicate that a statement is not totally true or not true in every place and time. An absolute statement will contain no hedges, but in many subjects, the answers are not always straightforward or absolute. There are always exceptions to the rules in these subjects. For this reason,

you should favor those multiple-choice questions that contain hedging language. The presence of qualifying words indicates that the author is taking special care with his or her words, which is certainly important when composing the right answer. After all, there are many ways to be wrong, but there is only one way to be right! For this reason, it is wise to avoid answers that are absolute when taking a multiple-choice test. An absolute answer is one that says things are either all one way or all another. They often include words like *every*, *always*, *best*, and *never*. If you are taking a multiple-choice test in a subject that doesn't lend itself to absolute answers, be on your guard if you see any of these words.

12. Long Answers

In many subject areas, the answers are not simple. As already mentioned, the right answer often requires hedges. Another common feature of the answers to a complex or subjective question are qualifying clauses, which are groups of words that subtly modify the meaning of the sentence. If the question or answer choice describes a rule to which there are exceptions or the subject matter is complicated, ambiguous, or confusing, the correct answer will require many words in order to be expressed clearly and accurately. In essence, you should not be deterred by answer choices that seem excessively long. Oftentimes, the author of the text will not be able to write the correct answer without offering some qualifications and modifications. Your job is to read the answer choices thoroughly and completely and to select the one that most accurately and precisely answers the question.

13. Restating to Understand

Sometimes, a question on a multiple-choice test is difficult not because of what it asks but because of how it is written. If this is the case, restate the question or answer choice in different words. This process serves a couple of important purposes. First, it forces you to concentrate on the core of the question. In order to rephrase the question accurately, you have to understand it well. Rephrasing the question will concentrate your mind on the key words and ideas. Second, it will present the information to your mind in a fresh way. This process may trigger your memory and render some useful scrap of information picked up while studying.

14. True Statements

Sometimes an answer choice will be true in itself, but it does not answer the question. This is one of the main reasons why it is essential to read the question carefully and completely before proceeding to the answer choices. Too often, test takers skip ahead to the answer choices and look for true statements. Having found one of these, they are content to select it without reference to the question above. The savvy test taker will always read the entire question before turning to the answer choices. Then, having settled on a correct answer choice, he or she will refer to the original question and ensure that the selected answer is relevant. The mistake of choosing a correct-but-irrelevant answer choice is especially common on questions related to specific pieces of objective knowledge.

15. No Patterns

One of the more dangerous ideas that circulates about multiple-choice tests is that the correct answers tend to fall into patterns. These erroneous ideas range from a belief that B and C are the most common right answers, to the idea that an unprepared test-taker should answer "A-B-A-C-A-D-A-B-A." It cannot be emphasized enough that pattern-seeking of this type is exactly the WRONG way to approach a multiple-choice test. To begin with, it is highly unlikely that the test maker will plot the correct answers according to some predetermined pattern. The questions are scrambled and delivered in a random order. Furthermore, even if the test maker was following a pattern in the assignation of correct answers, there is no reason why the test taker would know which pattern he or she was using. Any attempt to discern a pattern in the answer choices is a waste of time and a distraction from the real work of taking the test. A test taker would be much better served by extra preparation before the test than by reliance on a pattern in the answers.

Introduction to the CJBAT

Function of the Test

The Criminal Justice Basic Abilities Test (CJBAT) is an exam given to those who wish to become police or correctional officers. The exam measures the "minimum competencies" it would take to become certified law enforcement and is developed by Industrial/Organizational Solutions (IOS) Inc. The CJBAT is given only in Florida with exam pass/fail results given to applicants, training schools, and criminal justice agencies via the Florida Department of Law Enforcement website.

Test Administration

The CJBAT is offered in the state of Florida and is administered by Pearson VUE through a Pearson testing center or an affiliate assessment center. Those who wish to schedule their CJBAT should go to the Pearson website where they will be given the dates and times of available exams. Those who wish to retake the CJBAT have three attempts to do so within a twelve-month period. Otherwise, test takers must wait until the next year to schedule another exam. Any test accommodations must be made in request through the Pearson VUE website.

Test Format

On exam day, test takers should bring two forms of ID, one of the forms being a government-issued photo ID, like an ID or passport. Electronic devices are not allowed at the testing site, and there is also no storage at the testing site. Any materials such as purses or phones will be collected and then returned to you after the exam is completed. Eating, drinking, and smoking is not allowed.

There are 97 questions on the CJBAT in total, and test takers have 90 minutes to complete the exam. The exam will be at a computer-based testing site. There are three sections on the CJBAT, listed below:

- Section I: Behavioral attributes; 47 questions; 20 minutes
    - The behavioral attributes section will ask questions about your reaction or belief about a situation wherein you "strongly agree, agree, unsure, disagree, or strongly disagree" with a statement using the numbers 1 through 5.

- Section II: Memorization; 10 questions; 2 ½ minutes
    - For this section, test takers have one minute to review an image and then one and a half minutes to answer the questions after the image is taken away.

- Section III: Written comprehension, written expression, and reasoning (deductive and inductive); 40 questions; 60 minutes
    - This section measures cognitive abilities and contains 40 questions.

Scoring

A passing score on the CJBAT is a 70 or higher across all sections. Test takers must also pass 30 of the 50 items located on Sections II and III. A pass/fail will be given to test takers after they have finished rather than an actual numerical score.

Study Prep Plan for the CJBAT

1 **Schedule** - Use one of our study schedules below or come up with one of your own.

2 **Relax** - Test anxiety can hurt even the best students. There are many ways to reduce stress. Find the one that works best for you.

3 **Execute** - Once you have a good plan in place, be sure to stick to it.

One Week Study Schedule

Day 1	Written Comprehension
Day 2	Written Expression
Day 3	Memorization
Day 4	Personal Characteristics/Behavioral Attributes
Day 5	Practice Test #1
Day 6	Practice Test #2
Day 7	Take Your Exam!

Two Week Study Schedule

Day 1	Written Comprehension	Day 8	Practice Test #1
Day 2	Inferences in a Text	Day 9	Answer Explanations #1
Day 3	Written Expression	Day 10	Practice Test #2
Day 4	Sentence Structures	Day 11	Answer Explanations #2
Day 5	Memorization	Day 12	Practice Test #3
Day 6	Reasoning	Day 13	Answer Explanations #3
Day 7	Personal Characteristics/ Behavioral Attributes	Day 14	Take Your Exam!

Build your own prep plan by visiting:

testprepbooks.com/prep

Written Comprehension

Literary Analysis

Purpose of a Passage

When it comes to an author's writing, readers should always identify a purpose. No matter how objective a text may seem, readers should assume the author has preconceived beliefs. One can reduce the likelihood of accepting an invalid argument by looking for multiple articles on the topic, including those with varying opinions. If several opinions point in the same direction and are backed by reputable peer-reviewed sources, it's more likely the author has a valid argument. Positions that run contrary to widely held beliefs and existing data should invite scrutiny. There are exceptions to the rule, so be a careful consumer of information.

Though themes, symbols, and motifs are buried deep within the text and can sometimes be difficult to infer, an **author's purpose** is usually obvious from the beginning. No matter the genre or format, all authors are writing to persuade, inform, or entertain. Often, these purposes are blended, with one dominating the rest. It's useful to learn to recognize the author's intent.

Persuasive writing is used to persuade or convince readers of something. It often contains two elements: the argument and the counterargument. The argument takes a stance on an issue, while the counterargument pokes holes in the opposition's stance. Authors rely on logic, emotion, and writer credibility to persuade readers to agree with them. If readers are opposed to the stance before reading, they are unlikely to adopt that stance. However, those who are undecided or committed to the same stance are more likely to agree with the author.

Informative writing tries to teach or inform. Workplace manuals, instructor lessons, statistical reports and cookbooks are examples of informative texts. Informative writing is usually based on facts and void of emotion and persuasion. Informative texts generally contain statistics, charts, and graphs. Though most informative texts lack a persuasive agenda, readers must examine the text carefully to determine whether one exists within a given passage.

Stories or narratives are designed to entertain. When people go to the movies, it's usually to escape for a few hours, not to think critically. Narrative writing is designed to delight and engage the reader. However, sometimes this type of writing can be woven into more serious materials, such as persuasive or informative writing to hook the reader before transitioning into a more scholarly discussion.

Emotional writing works to evoke the reader's feelings, such as anger, euphoria, or sadness. The connection between reader and author is an attempt to cause the reader to share the author's intended emotion or tone. Sometimes in order to make a piece more poignant, the author simply wants readers to feel the same emotions that the author has felt. Other times, the author attempts to persuade or manipulate the reader into adopting his stance. While it's okay to sympathize with the author, be aware of the individual's underlying intent.

The various writing styles are usually blended, with one purpose dominating the rest. A persuasive text, for example, might begin with a humorous tale to make readers more receptive to the persuasive message, or a recipe in a cookbook designed to inform might be preceded by an entertaining anecdote that makes the recipes more appealing.

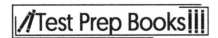

Text Structure

Depending on what the author is attempting to accomplish, certain formats or text structures work better than others. For example, a sequence structure might work for narration but not when identifying similarities and differences between dissimilar concepts. Similarly, a comparison-contrast structure is not useful for narration. It's the author's job to put the right information in the correct format.

Readers should be familiar with the five main literary structures:

1. **Sequence structure** (sometimes referred to as the order structure) is when the order of events proceed in a predictable order. In many cases, this means the text goes through the plot elements: exposition, rising action, climax, falling action, and resolution. Readers are introduced to characters, setting, and conflict in the **exposition**. In the **rising action**, there's an increase in tension and suspense. The **climax** is the height of tension and the point of no return. **Tension** decreases during the falling action. In the **resolution**, any conflicts presented in the exposition are solved, and the story concludes. An informative text that is structured sequentially will often go in order from one step to the next.

2. In the **problem-solution structure**, authors identify a potential problem and suggest a solution. This form of writing is usually divided into two parts (the problem and the solution) and can be found in informational texts. For example, cell phone, cable, and satellite providers use this structure in manuals to help customers troubleshoot or identify problems with services or products.

3. When authors want to discuss similarities and differences between separate concepts, they arrange thoughts in a **comparison-contrast paragraph structure**. Venn diagrams are an effective graphic organizer for comparison-contrast structures because they feature two overlapping circles that can be used to organize similarities and differences. A comparison-contrast essay organizes one paragraph based on similarities and another based on differences. A comparison-contrast essay can also be arranged with the similarities and differences of individual traits addressed within individual paragraphs. Words such as *however*, *but*, and *nevertheless* help signal a contrast in ideas.

4. **Descriptive writing structure** is designed to appeal to your senses. Much like an artist who constructs a painting, good descriptive writing builds an image in the reader's mind by appealing to the five senses: sight, hearing, taste, touch, and smell. However, overly descriptive writing can become tedious, whereas sparse descriptions can make settings and characters seem flat. Good authors strike a balance by applying descriptions only to passages, characters, and settings that are integral to the plot.

5. Passages that use the **cause-and-effect** structure are asking why (the cause) and what (the effect). Words such as *if*, *since*, *because*, *then*, or *consequently* indicate relationship. By switching the order of a complex sentence, the writer can rearrange the emphasis on different clauses. Saying *If Sheryl is late, we'll miss the dance* is different from saying *We'll miss the dance if Sheryl is late*. One emphasizes Sheryl's tardiness while the other emphasizes missing the dance. Paragraphs can also be arranged in a cause-and-effect format. Cause and effect writing discusses the impact of decisions that have been made or could be made. Researchers often apply this paragraph structure to the scientific method.

Point of View

Point of view is an important writing device to consider. In fiction writing, point of view refers to who tells the story or from whose perspective readers are observing the story. In nonfiction writing, the

Written Comprehension

point of view refers to whether the author refers to himself/herself, his/her readers, or chooses not to mention either. Whether fiction or nonfiction, the author will carefully consider the impact the perspective will have on the purpose and main point of the writing.

- **First-person point of view**: The story is told from the writer's perspective. In fiction, this would mean that the main character is also the narrator. First-person point of view is easily recognized by the use of personal pronouns such as *I*, *me*, *we*, *us*, *our*, *my*, and *myself*.

- **Third-person point of view**: In a more formal essay, this would be an appropriate perspective because the focus should be on the subject matter, not the writer or the reader. Third-person point of view is recognized by the use of the pronouns *he*, *she*, *they*, and *it*. In fiction writing, third-person point of view has a few variations.

  - **Third-person limited** point of view refers to a story told by a narrator who has access to the thoughts and feelings of just one character.

  - In **third-person omniscient** point of view, the narrator has access to the thoughts and feelings of all the characters.

  - In **third-person objective** point of view, the narrator is like a fly on the wall and can see and hear what the characters do and say but does not have access to their thoughts and feelings.

- **Second-person point of view**: This point of view isn't commonly used in fiction or nonfiction writing because it directly addresses the reader using the pronouns *you*, *your*, and *yourself*. Second-person perspective is more appropriate in direct communication, such as business letters or emails.

Point of View	Pronouns Used
First person	I, me, we, us, our, my, myself
Second person	You, your, yourself
Third person	He, she, it, they

Style, Tone, and Mood

Style, tone, and mood are often thought to be the same thing. Though they're closely related, there are important differences to keep in mind. The easiest way to do this is to remember that style "creates and affects" tone and mood. More specifically, style is how the writer uses words to create the desired tone and mood for their writing.

Style

Style can include any number of technical writing choices. A few examples of style choices include:

- **Sentence construction**: When presenting facts, does the writer use shorter sentences to create a quicker sense of the supporting evidence, or do they use longer sentences to elaborate and explain the information?

- **Technical language**: Does the writer use jargon to demonstrate their expertise in the subject, or do they use ordinary language to help the reader understand things in simple terms?

- **Formal language**: Does the writer use a conversational style of writing to connect to the reader, or do they withhold using contractions such as *don't* or *shouldn't* in order to create a more formal tone?

- **Formatting**: Does the writer use a series of shorter paragraphs to help the reader follow a line of argument, or do they use longer paragraphs to examine an issue in great detail and demonstrate their knowledge of the topic?

On the test, examine the writer's style and how their writing choices affect the way the text comes across.

Tone

Tone refers to the writer's attitude toward the subject matter. Tone conveys how the writer feels about characters, situations, events, ideas, etc. For example, the tone conveys how the writer feels about their characters and the situations in which they're involved.

A lot of nonfiction writing has a neutral tone, which is an important tone for the writer to take. A neutral tone demonstrates that the writer is presenting a topic impartially and letting the information speak for itself. On the other hand, nonfiction writing can be just as effective and appropriate if the tone isn't neutral. For instance, take this example involving seat belts:

> Seat belts save more lives than any other automobile safety feature. Many studies show that airbags save lives as well; however, not all cars have airbags. For instance, some older cars don't. Furthermore, air bags aren't entirely reliable. For example, studies show that in 15% of accidents airbags don't deploy as designed, but, on the other hand, seat belt malfunctions are extremely rare. The number of highway fatalities has plummeted since laws requiring seat belt usage were enacted.

In this passage, the writer mostly chooses to retain a neutral tone when presenting information. If the writer would instead include their own personal experience of losing a friend or family member in a car accident, the tone would change dramatically. The tone would no longer be neutral and would show that the writer has a personal stake in the content, allowing them to interpret the information in a different way. When analyzing tone, consider what the writer is trying to achieve in the text and how they *create* the tone using style.

Mood

Mood refers to the feelings and atmosphere that the writer's words create for the reader. Like tone, many nonfiction texts can have a neutral mood. To return to the previous example, if the writer would choose to include information about a person they know being killed in a car accident, the text would suddenly carry an emotional component that is absent in the previous example. Depending on how they present the information, the writer can create a sad, angry, or even hopeful mood. When analyzing the mood, consider what the writer wants to accomplish and whether the best choice was made to achieve that end.

Consistency

Whatever style, tone, and mood the writer uses, good writing should remain consistent throughout. If the writer chooses to include the tragic, personal experience above, it would affect the style, tone, and mood of the entire text. It would seem out of place for such an example to be used in the middle of a neutral, measured, and analytical text. To adjust the rest of the text, the writer needs to make additional choices to remain consistent. For example, the writer might decide to use the word *tragedy* in place of the more neutral *fatality*, or they could describe a series of car-related deaths as an *epidemic*. Adverbs and adjectives such as *devastating* or *horribly* could be included to maintain this consistent attitude toward the content. When analyzing writing, look for sudden shifts in style, tone, and mood, and consider whether the writer would be wiser to maintain the prevailing strategy.

Influences of Historical Context

Studying historical literature is fascinating. It reveals a snapshot in time of people, places, and cultures; a collective set of beliefs and attitudes that no longer exist. Writing changes as attitudes and cultures evolve. Beliefs previously considered immoral or wrong may be considered acceptable today. Researching the historical period of an author gives the reader perspective. The dialogue in Jane Austen's *Pride and Prejudice*, for example, is indicative of social class during the Regency era. Similarly, the stereotypes and slurs in *The Adventures of Huckleberry Finn* were a result of common attitudes and beliefs in the late 1800s, attitudes now found to be reprehensible.

Recognizing Cultural Themes

Regardless of culture, place, or time, certain themes are universal to the human condition. Because humans experience joy, rage, jealousy, and pride, certain themes span centuries. For example, Shakespeare's *Macbeth,* as well as modern works like *The 50th Law* by rapper 50 Cent and Robert Greene or the Netflix series *House of Cards* all feature characters who commit atrocious acts because of ambition. Similarly, *The Adventures of Huckleberry Finn*, published in the 1880s, and *The Catcher in the Rye*, published in the 1950s, both have characters who lie, connive, and survive on their wits.

Moviegoers know whether they are seeing an action, romance or horror film, and are often disappointed if the movie doesn't fit into the conventions of a particular category. Similarly, categories or genres give readers a sense of what to expect from a text. Some of the most basic genres in literature include books, short stories, poetry, and drama. Many genres can be split into sub-genres. For example, the sub-genres of historical fiction, realistic fiction, and fantasy all fit under the fiction genre.

Each genre has a unique way of approaching a particular theme. Books and short stories use plot, characterization, and setting, while poems rely on figurative language, sound devices, and symbolism. Dramas reveal plot through dialogue and the actor's voice and body language.

Main Ideas and Supporting Details

It is very important to know the difference between the topic and the main idea of the text. Even though these two are similar because they both present the central point of a text, they have distinctive differences. A **topic** is the subject of the text; This can usually be described in a concise one- to two-word phrase. On the other hand, the **main idea** is more detailed and provides the author's central point of the text. It can be expressed through a complete sentence and can be found in the beginning, middle, or end of a paragraph. In most nonfiction books, the first sentence of the passage usually (but not always) states the main idea. Take a look at the passage below to review the topic versus the main idea:

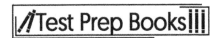

> Cheetahs are one of the fastest mammals on land, reaching up to 70 miles an hour over short distances. Even though cheetahs can run as fast as 70 miles an hour, they usually only have to run half that speed to catch up with their choice of prey. Cheetahs cannot maintain a fast pace over long periods of time because they will overheat their bodies. After a chase, cheetahs need to rest for approximately 30 minutes prior to eating or returning to any other activity.

In the example above, the topic of the passage is "Cheetahs" simply because that is the subject of the text. The main idea of the text is "Cheetahs are one of the fastest mammals on land but can only maintain this fast pace for short distances." While it covers the topic, it is more detailed and refers to the text in its entirety.

Supporting Details

Supporting details help readers better develop and understand the main idea. Supporting details answer questions like *who, what, where, when, why,* and *how.* Different types of supporting details include examples, facts and statistics, anecdotes, and sensory details.

Persuasive and informative texts often use supporting details. In persuasive texts, authors attempt to make readers agree with their point of view, and supporting details are often used as "selling points." If authors make a statement, they should support the statement with evidence in order to adequately persuade readers. Informative texts use supporting details such as examples and facts to inform readers. Take another look at the previous "Cheetahs" passage to find examples of supporting details:

> Cheetahs are one of the fastest mammals on land, reaching up to 70 miles an hour over short distances. Even though cheetahs can run as fast as 70 miles an hour, they usually only have to run half that speed to catch up with their choice of prey. Cheetahs cannot maintain a fast pace over long periods of time because they will overheat their bodies. After a chase, cheetahs need to rest for approximately 30 minutes prior to eating or returning to any other activity.

In the example above, supporting details include:

- Cheetahs reach up to 70 miles per hour over short distances.
- They usually only have to run half that speed to catch up with their prey.
- Cheetahs will overheat their bodies if they exert a high speed over longer distances.
- Cheetahs need to rest for 30 minutes after a chase.

Drawing Conclusions

Determining conclusions requires being an active reader, as a reader must make a prediction and analyze facts to identify a conclusion. There are a few ways to determine a logical conclusion, but careful reading is the most important. It's helpful to read a passage a few times, noting details that seem important to the piece. A reader should also identify key words in a passage to determine the logical conclusion or determination that flows from the information presented.

Textual evidence within the details helps readers draw a conclusion about a passage. **Textual evidence** refers to information—facts and examples that support the main point. Textual evidence will likely come from outside sources and can be in the form of quoted or paraphrased material. In order to draw a conclusion from evidence, it's important to examine the credibility and validity of that evidence as well as how (and if) it relates to the main idea.

Written Comprehension

If an author presents a differing opinion or a **counter-argument** in order to refute it, the reader should consider how and why this information is being presented. It is meant to strengthen the original argument and shouldn't be confused with the author's intended conclusion, but it should also be considered in the reader's final evaluation.

Sometimes, authors explicitly state the conclusion they want readers to understand. Alternatively, a conclusion may not be directly stated. In that case, readers must rely on the implications to form a logical conclusion:

> On the way to the bus stop, Michael realized his homework wasn't in his backpack. He ran back to the house to get it and made it back to the bus just in time.

In this example, though it's never explicitly stated, it can be inferred that Michael is a student on his way to school in the morning. When forming a conclusion from implied information, it's important to read the text carefully to find several pieces of evidence to support the conclusion.

Summarizing is an effective way to draw a conclusion from a passage. A **summary** is a shortened version of the original text, written by the reader in his/her own words. Focusing on the main points of the original text and including only the relevant details can help readers reach a conclusion. It's important to retain the original meaning of the passage.

Like summarizing, paraphrasing can also help a reader fully understand different parts of a text. **Paraphrasing** calls for the reader to take a small part of the passage and list or describe its main points. Paraphrasing is more than rewording the original passage, though. It should be written in the reader's own words, while still retaining the meaning of the original source. This will indicate an understanding of the original source, yet still help the reader expand on his/her interpretation.

Readers should pay attention to the **sequence**, or the order in which details are laid out in the text, as this can be important to understanding its meaning as a whole. Writers will often use transitional words to help the reader understand the order of events and to stay on track. Words like *next, then, after*, and *finally* show that the order of events is important to the author. In some cases, the author omits these transitional words, and the sequence is implied. Authors may even purposely present the information out of order to make an impact or have an effect on the reader. An example might be when a narrative writer uses **flashback** to reveal information.

There are several ways readers can draw conclusions from authors' ideas, such as note taking, text evidence, text credibility, writing a response to text, directly stated information versus implications, outlining, summarizing, and paraphrasing. Let's take a look at each important strategy to help readers draw logical conclusions.

Note Taking

When readers **take notes** throughout texts or passages, they are jotting down important facts or points that the author makes. Note taking is a useful record of information that helps readers understand the text or passage and respond to it. When taking notes, readers should keep lines brief and filled with pertinent information so that they are not rereading a large amount of text, but rather just key points, elements, or words. After readers have completed a text or passage, they can refer to their notes to help them form a conclusion about the author's ideas in the text or passage.

Text Evidence

Text evidence is the information readers find in a text or passage that supports the main idea or point(s) in a story. In turn, text evidence can help readers draw conclusions about the text or passage. The information should be taken directly from the text or passage and placed in quotation marks. Text evidence provides readers with information to support ideas about the text so that they do not rely simply on their own thoughts. Details should be precise, descriptive, and factual. Statistics are a great piece of text evidence because they provide readers with exact numbers and not just a generalization. For example, instead of saying "Asia has a larger population than Europe," authors could provide detailed information such as, "In Asia there are over 4 billion people, whereas in Europe there are a little over 750 million." More definitive information provides better evidence to readers to help support their conclusions about texts or passages.

Text Credibility

Credible sources are important when drawing conclusions because readers need to be able to trust what they are reading. Authors should always use credible sources to help gain the trust of their readers. A text is **credible** when it is believable and the author is objective and unbiased. If readers do not trust an author's words, they may simply dismiss the text completely. For example, if an author writes a persuasive essay, he or she is outwardly trying to sway readers' opinions to align with his or her own. Readers may agree or disagree with the author, which may, in turn, lead them to believe that the author is credible or not credible. Also, readers should keep in mind the source of the text. If readers review a journal about astronomy, would a more reliable source be a NASA employee or a medical doctor? Overall, text credibility is important when drawing conclusions, because readers want reliable sources that support the decisions they have made about the author's ideas.

Writing a Response to Text

Once readers have determined their opinions and validated the credibility of a text, they can then reflect on the text. Writing a response to a text is one way readers can reflect on the given text or passage. When readers write responses to a text, it is important for them to rely on the evidence within the text to support their opinions or thoughts. Supporting evidence such as facts, details, statistics, and quotes directly from the text are key pieces of information readers should reflect upon or use when writing a response to text.

Directly Stated Information Versus Implications

Engaged readers should constantly self-question while reviewing texts to help them form conclusions. Self-questioning is when readers review a paragraph, page, passage, or chapter and ask themselves, "Did I understand what I read?," "What was the main event in this section?," "Where is this taking place?," and so on. Authors can provide clues or pieces of evidence throughout a text or passage to guide readers toward a conclusion. This is why active and engaged readers should read the text or passage in its entirety before forming a definitive conclusion. If readers do not gather all the pieces of evidence needed, then they may jump to an illogical conclusion.

At times, authors directly state conclusions while others simply imply them. Of course, it is easier if authors outwardly provide conclusions to readers because it does not leave any information open to interpretation. On the other hand, implications are things that authors do not directly state but can be assumed based off of information they provided. If authors only imply what may have happened, readers can form a menagerie of ideas for conclusions. For example, look at the following statement: "Once we heard the sirens, we hunkered down in the storm shelter." In this statement, the author does

Written Comprehension

not directly state that there was a tornado, but clues such as "sirens" and "storm shelter" provide insight to the readers to help form that conclusion.

<u>Outlining</u>

An **outline** is a system used to organize writing. When reading texts, outlining is important because it helps readers organize important information in a logical pattern using roman numerals. Usually, outlines start with the main idea(s) and then branch out into subgroups or subsidiary thoughts of subjects. Not only do outlines provide a visual tool for readers to reflect on how events, characters, settings, or other key parts of the text or passage relate to one another, but they can also lead readers to a stronger conclusion.

The sample below demonstrates what a general outline looks like.

I. Main Topic 1
    a. Subtopic 1
    b. Subtopic 2
        1. Detail 1
        2. Detail 2
II. Main Topic 2
    a. Subtopic 1
    b. Subtopic 2
        1. Detail 1
        2. Detail 2

Inferences in a Text

Readers should be able to make inferences. **Making an inference** requires the reader to read between the lines and look for what is implied rather than what is directly stated. That is, using information that is known from the text, the reader is able to make a logical assumption about information that is *not* directly stated but is probably true. Read the following passage:

"Hey, do you want to meet my new puppy?" Jonathan asked.

"Oh, I'm sorry but please don't—" Jacinta began to protest, but before she could finish, Jonathan had already opened the passenger side door of his car and a perfect white ball of fur came bouncing towards Jacinta.

"Isn't he the cutest?" beamed Jonathan.

"Yes—achoo!—he's pretty—aaaachooo!!—adora—aaa—aaaachoo!" Jacinta managed to say in between sneezes. "But if you don't mind, I—I—achoo!—need to go inside."

Which of the following can be inferred from Jacinta's reaction to the puppy?
   a. She hates animals.
   b. She is allergic to dogs.
   c. She prefers cats to dogs.
   d. She is angry at Jonathan.

An inference requires the reader to consider the information presented and then form their own idea about what is probably true. Based on the details in the passage, what is the best answer to the question? Important details to pay attention to in the passage include the tone of Jacinta's dialogue, as well as her reaction itself, which is a long string of sneezes. Answer choices (a) and (d) both express strong emotions ("hates" and "angry") that are not evident in Jacinta's speech or actions. Answer choice (c) mentions cats, but there is nothing in the passage to indicate Jacinta's feelings about cats. Answer choice (b), "she is allergic to dogs," is the most logical choice. Based on the fact she began sneezing as soon as a fluffy dog approached her, it makes sense to guess that Jacinta might be allergic to dogs. Using the clues in the passage, it is reasonable to guess that this is true even though Jacinta never directly states, "Sorry, I'm allergic to dogs!"

Making inferences is crucial because literary texts often avoid presenting complete and direct information to readers about characters' thoughts or feelings, or they present the information in an unclear way, leaving it up to the reader to interpret clues given in the text. In order to make inferences while reading, readers should ask themselves:

- What details are being presented in the text?
- Is there any important information that seems to be missing?
- Based on the information that the author *does* include, what else is probably true?
- Is this inference reasonable based on what is already known?

Apply Information

A natural extension of making inferences is also being able to apply that information to new contexts. This is especially useful in nonfiction or informative writing. Considering the facts and details presented in the text, readers should consider how the same information might be relevant in a different situation. The following is an example of applying an inferential conclusion to a different context:

> Often, individuals behave differently in large groups than they do as individuals. One example of this is the psychological phenomenon known as the bystander effect. According to the bystander effect, the more people who witness an accident or crime occur, the less likely each individual bystander is to respond or offer assistance to the victim. A classic example of this is the murder of Kitty Genovese in New York City in the 1960s. Although there were over thirty witnesses to her killing by a stabber, none of them intervened to help Kitty or contact the police.

Considering the phenomenon of the bystander effect, what would probably happen if somebody tripped on the stairs in a crowded subway station?
   a. Everybody would stop to help the person who tripped
   b. Bystanders would point and laugh at the person who tripped
   c. Someone would call the police after walking away from the station
   d. Few if any bystanders would offer assistance to the person who tripped

Written Comprehension

This question asks readers to apply the information they learned from the passage, which is an informative paragraph about the bystander effect. According to the passage, this is a concept in psychology that describes the way people in groups respond to an accident—the more people that are present, the less likely any one person is to intervene. While the passage illustrates this effect with the example of a woman's murder, the question asks readers to apply it to a different context—in this case, someone falling down the stairs in front of many subway passengers. Although this specific situation is not discussed in the passage, readers should be able to apply the general concepts described in the paragraph. The definition of the bystander effect includes any instance of an accident or crime in front of a large group of people. The question asks about a situation that falls within the same definition, so the general concept should still hold true: in the midst of a large crowd, few individuals are likely to actually respond to an accident. In this case, answer choice (d) is the best response.

Critical Thinking Skills

It's important to read any piece of writing critically. The goal is to discover the point and purpose of what the author is writing about through analysis. It's also crucial to establish the point or stance the author has taken on the topic of the piece. After determining the author's perspective, readers can then more effectively develop their own viewpoints on the subject of the piece.

It is important to distinguish between fact and opinion when reading a piece of writing. A **fact** is information that is true. If information can be disproven, it is not a fact. For example, water freezes at or below thirty-two degrees Fahrenheit. An argument stating that water freezes at seventy degrees Fahrenheit cannot be supported by data and is therefore not a fact. Facts tend to be associated with science, mathematics, and statistics. **Opinions** are information open for debate. Opinions are often tied to subjective concepts like feelings, desires, or manners. They can also be controversial.

Authors often use words like *think, feel, believe,* or *in my opinion* when expressing opinion, but these words won't always appear in an opinion piece, especially if it is formally written. An author's opinion may be backed up by facts, which gives it more credibility, but that opinion should not be taken as fact. A critical reader should be suspect of an author's opinion, especially if it is only supported by other opinions.

Fact	Opinion
There are 9 innings in a game of baseball.	Baseball games run too long.
James Garfield was assassinated on July 2, 1881.	James Garfield was a good president.
McDonalds has stores in 118 countries.	McDonalds has the best hamburgers.

Critical readers examine the facts used to support an author's argument. They check the facts against other sources to be sure those facts are correct. They also check the validity of the sources used to be sure those sources are credible, academic, and/or peer reviewed. Consider that when an author uses another person's opinion to support his or her argument, even if it is an expert's opinion, it is still only an opinion and should not be taken as fact. A strong argument uses valid, measurable facts to support ideas. Even then, the reader may disagree with the argument as it may be rooted in his or her personal beliefs.

An authoritative argument may use the facts to sway the reader. Because of this, a writer may choose to only use the information and expert opinion that supports his or her viewpoint.

If the argument is that wind energy is the best solution, the author will use facts that support this idea. That same author may leave out relevant facts on solar energy. The way the author uses facts can influence the reader, so it's important to consider the facts being used, how those facts are being presented, and what information might be left out.

Critical readers should also look for errors in the argument such as logical fallacies and bias. A **logical fallacy** is a flaw in the logic used to make the argument. Logical fallacies include slippery slope, straw man, and begging the question. Authors can also reflect **bias** if they ignore an opposing viewpoint or present their side in an unbalanced way. A strong argument considers the opposition and finds a way to refute it. Critical readers should look for an unfair or one-sided presentation of the argument and be skeptical, as a bias may be present. Even if this bias is unintentional, if it exists in the writing, the reader should be wary of the validity of the argument.

Readers should also look for the use of **stereotypes**. These are the overly simplified beliefs about a person, place, thing, etc. that is indiscriminately applied to a larger group. These can be positive but are usually negative in nature. When a reader comes across the use of stereotypes, they should take that into consideration as they analyze the author's argument. These should generally be avoided. Stereotypes reveal a flaw in the writer's thinking and may suggest a lack of knowledge or understanding about the subject.

Author's Use of Language

Authors utilize a wide range of techniques to tell a story or communicate information. Readers should be familiar with the most common of these techniques. Techniques of writing are also commonly known as **rhetorical devices**.

Types of Appeals

In nonfiction writing, authors employ argumentative techniques to present their opinion to readers in the most convincing way. Persuasive writing usually includes at least one type of appeal: an appeal to logic (logos), emotion (pathos), or credibility and trustworthiness (ethos). When a writer appeals to logic, they are asking readers to agree with them based on research, evidence, and an established line of reasoning. An author's argument might also appeal to readers' emotions, perhaps by including personal stories and anecdotes (a short narrative of a specific event). A final type of appeal, appeal to authority, asks the reader to agree with the author's argument on the basis of their expertise or credentials. Consider three different approaches to arguing the same opinion:

<u>Logic (Logos)</u>
This is an example of an appeal to logic:

> Our school should abolish its current ban on cell phone use on campus. This rule was adopted last year as an attempt to reduce class disruptions and help students focus more on their lessons. However, since the rule was enacted, there has been no change in the number of disciplinary problems in class. Therefore, the rule is ineffective and should be done away with.

The author uses evidence to disprove the logic of the school's rule (the rule was supposed to reduce discipline problems, but the number of problems has not been reduced; therefore, the rule is not working) and call for its repeal.

Emotion (Pathos)

An author's argument might also appeal to readers' emotions, perhaps by including personal stories and anecdotes. The next example presents an appeal to emotion. By sharing the personal anecdote of one student and speaking about emotional topics like family relationships, the author invokes the reader's empathy in asking them to reconsider the school rule.

> Our school should abolish its current ban on cell phone use on campus. If they aren't able to use their phones during the school day, many students feel isolated from their loved ones. For example, last semester, one student's grandmother had a heart attack in the morning. However, because he couldn't use his cell phone, the student didn't know about his grandmother's accident until the end of the day—when she had already passed away, and it was too late to say goodbye. By preventing students from contacting their friends and family, our school is placing undue stress and anxiety on students.

Credibility (Ethos)

Finally, an appeal to authority includes a statement from a relevant expert. In this case, the author uses a doctor in the field of education to support the argument. All three examples begin from the same opinion—the school's phone ban needs to change—but rely on different argumentative styles to persuade the reader.

> Our school should abolish its current ban on cell phone use on campus. According to Dr. Bartholomew Everett, a leading educational expert, "Research studies show that cell phone usage has no real impact on student attentiveness. Rather, phones provide a valuable technological resource for learning. Schools need to learn how to integrate this new technology into their curriculum." Rather than banning phones altogether, our school should follow the advice of experts and allow students to use phones as part of their learning.

Rhetorical Questions

Another commonly used argumentative technique is asking rhetorical questions, questions that do not actually require an answer but that push the reader to consider the topic further.

> I wholly disagree with the proposal to ban restaurants from serving foods with high sugar and sodium contents. Do we really want to live in a world where the government can control what we eat? I prefer to make my own food choices.

Here, the author's rhetorical question prompts readers to put themselves in a hypothetical situation and imagine how they would feel about it.

Figurative Language

Literary texts also employ rhetorical devices. **Figurative language,** like the use of similes and metaphors, is a type of rhetorical device commonly found in literature. In addition to rhetorical devices that play on the *meanings* of words, there are also rhetorical devices that use the *sounds* of words. These devices are most often found in poetry but may also be found in other types of literature and in nonfiction writing like speech texts.

Alliteration and assonance are both varieties of sound repetition. Other types of sound repetition include: **anaphora**, repetition that occurs at the beginning of the sentences; **epiphora**, repetition occurring at the end of phrases; **antimetabole**, repetition of words in reverse order; and **antiphrasis**, a form of denial of an assertion in a text.

Alliteration refers to the repetition of the first sound of each word. Recall Robert Burns' opening line:

> My love is like a red, red rose

This line includes two instances of alliteration: "love" and "like" (repeated *L* sound), as well as "red" and "rose" (repeated *R* sound). Next, assonance refers to the repetition of vowel sounds and can occur anywhere within a word (not just the opening sound). Here is the opening of a poem by John Keats:

> When I have fears that I may cease to be
>
> Before my pen has glean'd my teeming brain

Assonance can be found in the words "fears," "cease," "be," "glean'd," and "teeming," all of which stress the long *E* sound. Both alliteration and assonance create a harmony that unifies the writer's language.

Another sound device is **onomatopoeia**, or words whose spelling mimics the sound they describe. Words such as "crash," "bang," and "sizzle" are all examples of onomatopoeia. Use of onomatopoetic language adds auditory imagery to the text.

Readers are probably most familiar with the technique of pun. A **pun** is a play on words, taking advantage of two words that have the same or similar pronunciation. Puns can be found throughout Shakespeare's plays, for instance:

> Now is the winter of our discontent
>
> Made glorious summer by this son of York

These lines from *Richard III* contain a play on words. Richard III refers to his brother, the newly crowned King Edward IV, as the "son of York," referencing their family heritage from the house of York. However, while drawing a comparison between the political climate and the weather (times of political trouble were the "winter," but now the new king brings "glorious summer"), Richard's use of the word "son" also implies another word with the same pronunciation, "sun"—so Edward IV is also like the sun, bringing light, warmth, and hope to England. Puns are a clever way for writers to suggest two meanings at once.

Counterarguments

If an author presents a differing opinion or a counterargument in order to refute it, the reader should consider how and why this information is being presented. It is meant to strengthen the original argument and shouldn't be confused with the author's intended conclusion, but it should also be considered in the reader's final evaluation.

Authors can exhibit bias if they ignore the opposing viewpoint or present their side in an unbalanced way. A strong argument considers the opposition and finds a way to refute it. Critical readers should look for an unfair or one-sided presentation of the argument and be skeptical, as a bias may be present. Even if this bias is unintentional, if it exists in the writing, the reader should be wary of the validity of the argument. Readers should also look for the use of stereotypes, which refer to specific groups.

Written Comprehension

Stereotypes are often negative connotations about a person or place and should always be avoided. When a critical reader finds stereotypes in a piece of writing, they should be critical of the argument and consider the validity of anything the author presents. Stereotypes reveal a flaw in the writer's thinking and may suggest a lack of knowledge or understanding about the subject.

Meaning of Words in Context

There will be many occasions in one's reading career in which an unknown word or a word with multiple meanings will pop up. There are ways of determining what these words or phrases mean that do not require the use of the dictionary, which is especially helpful during a test where one may not be available. Even outside of the exam, knowing how to derive an understanding of a word via context clues will be a critical skill in the real world. The context is the circumstances in which a story or a passage is happening, and can usually be found in the series of words directly before or directly after the word or phrase in question. The clues are the words that hint towards the meaning of the unknown word or phrase.

There may be questions that ask about the meaning of a particular word or phrase within a passage. There are a couple ways to approach these kinds of questions:

- Define the word or phrase in a way that is easy to comprehend (using context clues).
- Try out each answer choice in place of the word.

To demonstrate, here's an example from *Alice in Wonderland*:

> Alice was beginning to get very tired of sitting by her sister on the bank, and of having nothing to do: once or twice she peeped into the book her sister was reading, but it had no pictures or conversations in it, "and what is the use of a book," thought Alice, "without pictures or conversations?"

Q: As it is used in the selection, the word peeped means:

Using the first technique, before looking at the answers, define the word *peeped* using context clues and then find the matching answer. Then, analyze the entire passage in order to determine the meaning, not just the surrounding words.

To begin, imagine a blank where the word should be and put a synonym or definition there: "once or twice she _____ into the book her sister was reading." The context clue here is the book. It may be tempting to put *read* where the blank is, but notice the preposition word, *into*. One does not read *into* a book, one simply reads a book, and since reading a book requires that it is seen with a pair of eyes, then *look* would make the most sense to put into the blank: "once or twice she looked into the book her sister was reading."

Once an easy-to-understand word or synonym has been supplanted, readers should check to make sure it makes sense with the rest of the passage. What happened after she looked into the book? She thought to herself how a book without pictures or conversations is useless. This situation in its entirety makes sense.

Now check the answer choices for a match:
    a. To make a high-pitched cry
    b. To smack
    c. To look curiously
    d. To pout

Since the word was already defined, Choice *C* is the best option.

Using the second technique, replace the figurative blank with each of the answer choices and determine which one is the most appropriate. Remember to look further into the passage to clarify that they work, because they could still make sense out of context.
    a. Once or twice, she made a high pitched cry into the book her sister was reading
    b. Once or twice, she smacked into the book her sister was reading
    c. Once or twice, she looked curiously into the book her sister was reading
    d. Once or twice, she pouted into the book her sister was reading

For Choice *A*, it does not make much sense in any context for a person to cry into a book, unless maybe something terrible has happened in the story. Given that afterward Alice thinks to herself how useless a book without pictures is, this option does not make sense within context.

For Choice *B*, smacking a book someone is reading may make sense if the rest of the passage indicates a reason for doing so. If Alice was angry or her sister had shoved it in her face, then maybe smacking the book would make sense within context. However, since whatever she does with the book causes her to think, "what is the use of a book without pictures or conversations?" then answer Choice *B* is not an appropriate answer. Answer Choice *C* fits well within context, given her subsequent thoughts on the matter. Answer Choice *D* does not make sense in context or grammatically, as people do not pout into things.

This is a simple example to illustrate the techniques outlined above. There may, however, be a question in which all of the definitions are correct and also make sense out of context, in which the appropriate context clues will really need to be honed in on in order to determine the correct answer. For example, here is another passage from *Alice in Wonderland*:

> ... but when the Rabbit actually took a watch out of its waistcoat pocket, and looked at it, and then hurried on, Alice started to her feet, for it flashed across her mind that she had never before seen a rabbit with either a waistcoat-pocket or a watch to take out of it, and burning with curiosity, she ran across the field after it, and was just in time to see it pop down a large rabbit-hole under the hedge.

Q: As it is used in the passage, the word started means _____.
    a. to turn on
    b. to begin
    c. to move quickly
    d. to be surprised

All of these words qualify as a definition of *start*, but using context clues, the correct answer can be identified using one of the two techniques above. It's easy to see that one does not turn on, begin, or be surprised to one's feet. The selection also states that she "ran across the field after it," indicating that she was in a hurry. Therefore, to move quickly would make the most sense in this context.

Written Comprehension

The same strategies can be applied to vocabulary that may be completely unfamiliar. In this case, focus on the words before or after the unknown word in order to determine its definition. Take this sentence, for example:

> Sam was such a <u>miser</u> that he forced Andrew to pay him twelve cents for the candy, even though he had a large inheritance and he knew his friend was poor.

Unlike with assertion questions, for vocabulary questions, it may be necessary to apply some critical thinking skills when something isn't explicitly stated within the passage. Think about the implications of the passage, or what the text is trying to say. With this example, it is important to realize that it is considered unusually stingy for a person to demand so little money from someone instead of just letting their friend have the candy, especially if this person is already wealthy. Hence, a <u>miser</u> is a greedy or stingy individual.

Questions about complex vocabulary may not be explicitly asked, but this is a useful skill to know. If there is an unfamiliar word while reading a passage and its definition goes unknown, it is possible to miss out on a critical message that could inhibit the ability to appropriately answer the questions. Practicing this technique in daily life will sharpen this ability to derive meanings from context clues with ease.

Practice Quiz

The next two questions are based on the following passage:

> A drug-free school zone indicates an area where drug offenses carry stricter penalties. This policy was created in the 1970s to deter citizens from committing drug crimes on or around school grounds. A drug-free school zone is part of federal law, but states can vary the penalties enforced on those who are convicted of drug-related violations near school campuses. What constitutes a drug-free school zone is determined by each jurisdiction, but typically includes school grounds, adjacent areas within 1,000 feet, and school buses. Since the 1970s, all 50 states and Washington D.C. have adopted a drug-free school zone policy. More recently, some states have reduced the penalties, believing them to be too harsh for minor drug offenses that happened to occur near a school.

1. Based on the previous passage, which of the following statements best describes the purpose of a drug-free school zone?
    a. To help police locate and arrest students who are dealing drugs
    b. To help school staff to locate and eliminate the use of drugs on campus
    c. To deter people from committing drug-related crimes on and around schools
    d. To eliminate the use of drugs on school buses

2. Based on the previous passage, which of the following statements is most accurate?
    a. All fifty states have a 1000-foot zone around each school building that is designated as a Drug Free School Zone.
    b. The Drug Free School Zone enforces stricter penalties on those committed of drug-related offenses on or around school grounds.
    c. The Drug Free School Zone does not include school buses.
    d. Most states have abandoned the Drug Free School Zone policy because the penalties are too harsh.

The next two questions are based on the following passage:

> Any division of government (federal, state, or local) can declare a state of emergency. A state of emergency means that the government has suspended the normal constitutional procedures. In this case, citizens may not have the same rights that they typically do, such as driving on public roadways or whether they can remain in their homes. A state of emergency is typically declared in the wake of a disaster. Disasters can include hurricanes, tornadoes, floods, snowstorms, wildfires, and issues of public health such as a flu outbreak. In the event of a major snowstorm, for example, a government can issue a state of emergency to clear roads for emergency responders and to keep citizens safely in their homes. Declaring a state of emergency can also allow a government to access the use of funds, personnel, equipment, and supplies that are reserved for such a situation.

Written Comprehension

3. Based on the previous passage, which of the following statements best describes a state of emergency?
   a. The government suspends normal constitutional operations.
   b. Curfews are imposed by the government.
   c. All citizens must remain in their homes.
   d. The government can remove all citizens' rights.

4. Which of the following statements is most accurate based on the preceding passage?
   a. Declaring a state of emergency guarantees states will receive federal funding.
   b. Only state government can declare a state of emergency.
   c. Declaring a state of emergency allows the government to access reserved funding, personnel, and supplies.
   d. A state of emergency does not include issues of public health.

The next question is based on the following passage:

> In the event of a riot, police officers need to be prepared with the necessary gear to manage a large and potentially dangerous crowd. Front line riot police officers are equipped with helmets, riot shields, and body armor for protection. They also may carry gas masks in the event that tear gas is used to incapacitate or disperse a crowd. Riot police officers do have firearms, but less lethal methods of crowd management are preferred. Officers have traditionally used batons and whips to manage unruly crowds. In more recent years, police have begun using more effective methods, such as tear gas, pepper spray, tasers, and rubber bullets.

5. The main idea of this passage is best stated with which of the following sentences?
   a. Riot police use gas masks for protection from tear gas and pepper spray.
   b. Violent crowds should always be incapacitated with tear gas.
   c. Batons and whips are not very good methods of crowd control.
   d. Riot police must be prepared with the necessary equipment to manage a dangerous crowd.

See answers on next page.

Answer Explanations

1. C: Based on the passage, the best description of the purpose of a drug-free school zones is to deter citizens from committing drug related crimes on and around school campuses. Nothing in the passage suggests the law was created to help police identify students who are dealing drugs. The laws do not help schools identify drug use on campus; they only make penalties stricter for those who do. While a drug-free school zone may help deter drug use on school buses, this is not the primary purpose of the policy.

2. B: Based on the passage, the most accurate statement is that Drug Free School Zones enforce stricter penalties on those committing drug offenses on or near school grounds. While some states do enforce a 1000-foot zone around schools, the passage states that this is only typically the case, and is not the case for all fifty states. The Drug Free School Zone does include buses in most states. The passage notes that some states have reduced penalties in Drug Free School Zones, deeming them too harsh, but it does not say that most states have abandoned the policy.

3. A: The statement that best defines a state of emergency is the suspension of normal constitutional operation. While a curfew may be imposed when a state of emergency is declared, this is not always the case. Citizens may need to remain in their homes, but in the case of a hurricane or flood, evacuations may be necessary, so this answer is incorrect. While a government does have a right to alter citizens' rights in a state of emergency, it is to maintain their safety and does not extend to all of their rights as citizens.

4. C: Based on the passage, the best answer is that a state of emergency allows the government access to reserved supplies, funding, and personnel. The passage does not suggest that a state of emergency will guarantee federal funding to any government. Local, state, and federal government can declare a state of emergency. The passage states that issues of public health can be addressed with a state of emergency declaration.

5. D: This statement best captures the main idea, or main point of the paragraph, which is to show the necessary equipment police officers must have to best manage a riot. While riot police do use gas masks for protection, this is too specific to be the main idea of the paragraph. The passage mentions tear gas but does not suggest it is the best method to manage a crowd, so this is not the main focus of the paragraph. The passage does mention that better methods of crowd control than batons and whips have been used in recent years, but this is a supporting detail and not the main idea of the passage.

Written Expression

Spelling

Police officers are expected to express themselves with authority. Choosing the best words for each situation is only part of this task. Being able to spell those words correctly is also crucial. For this reason, their aptitude for spelling is measured on the exam. Consider, too, that accurate spelling helps to convey competence and professionalism.

Importance of Prefixes and Suffixes

The most common spelling mistakes are made when a **root word** (or a basic, core word) is modified by adding a prefix or a suffix to it. A **prefix** is a group of letters added to the beginning of a word, and a **suffix** is a group of letters added to the end of a word.

The prefixes usually change the meaning of the word. They might be negative or positive and signal time, location, or number. Note the spelling of the root word (or base word) does not change when adding a prefix.

Common Prefixes		
Prefix	**Meaning**	**Example**
dis-	not, opposite	disagree, disproportionate
en-, em-	to make, to cause	encode, embrace
in-, im-	in, into	induct
ir-, il-, im-	not, opposite	impossible, irresponsible
mis-	bad, wrongly	misfire, mistake
mono-	alone, one	monologue
non-	not, opposite	nonsense
over-	more than, too much	overlook
pre-	before	precede
post-	after	postmortem
re-	again, back	review
un-	not, opposite	unacceptable

A suffix can change the base word in two ways:

- Change numerical agreement: turns a singular word into a plural word (a singular witness becomes plural witnesses)

- Change grammatical function: turns one part of speech into another (noun to verb, verb to adverb), such as moderation, moderating, or moderately

Common Suffixes		
Suffix	Meaning/Use	Example
-able, -ible	able to	unbearable, plausible
-ance	state of being	significance
-al, -ial	relating to	lethal, testimonial, criminal
-ceed, -sede, -cede	go, go forward, withdraw, yield	exceed, recede, supersede
-ed	changes root word to past tense or past participle	called, played
-en	makes root word a verb	heighten, liven
-er	more, action, a person who does an action	clearer, sever, believer
-ful	full of	hateful, beautiful
-ian, -ite	person who does the action, part of a group	politician, meteorite
-ice, -ize	cause, treat, become	service, popularize
-ing	action	writing, playing
-ion, -tion	action or condition	celebration, organization
-ism	forms nouns referring to beliefs or behavior	Buddhism, recidivism
-ity, -ty	state of being	adversity, cruelty
-ive, -tive	state or quality	defensive, conservative
-less	without	tactless, nameless
-ly	in such a manner	poorly, happily
-ment	action	endorsement, disagreement
-ness	makes root word a noun referring to a state of being	weakness, kindness
-or	a person who does an action	moderator, perpetrator
-s, -es	makes root word plural	weights, boxes
-sion	state of being	admission, immersion
-y	made up of	moody, greasy

Doubling-Up Consonants (or Not)

When adding some suffixes (usually, *-ing, -sion*) to a root word that ends in one vowel followed immediately by one consonant, *double that last consonant*.

Base Word	Vowel/consonant	Suffix	Spelling Change
wrap	a, p	-ing	wrapping
canvas	a, s		canvassing
admit	i, t	-sion	admission

Written Expression

This rule does not apply to multi-vowel words, such as *sleep, treat,* and *appear.* When attaching a suffix that begins with a vowel to a word with a multi-letter vowel followed by a consonant, *do not double the consonant.*

Base Word	Multi-vowel, consonant	Suffix	Spelling
sleep	ee, p	-ing	sleeping
treat	ea, t	-ed	treated
appear	ea, r	-ance	appearance

Do *not* double the consonant if the root word already ends in a double consonant or the letter *x* (examples—*add/adding, fox/foxes*).

Words Ending with *y* or *c*

If a root word ends in a single vowel *y,* the *y* should be changed to i when adding any suffix, unless that suffix begins with the letter *i.* If a root word ends in a two-letter vowel, such as *oy, ay,* or *ey,* the *y* is kept.

Root Word	Ending	Suffix	Spelling Change
baby	y	-ed	babied
stymy	y	-ed	stymied
crony	y	-ism	cronyism
say	y	-ing	saying
annoy	oy	-ance	annoyance
survey	ey	-ing	surveying

In cases where the root word is a verb (ending with the letter *c*) and the suffix begins with an *e, i,* or *y,* the letter *k* is added to the end of the word between the last letter and the suffix.

Root Word	Ending	Suffix	Spelling Change
panic	ic	-ing	panicking
		-y	panicky
traffic	ic	-ed	trafficked
		-er	trafficker

Words with *ie* or *ei*

There's an old saying "*I* before *E,* except after *C.*" There's also a second part to it:

I before *E,*

Except after *C,*

Or when sounded as *A,*

As in *neighbor* and *weigh.*

Here are a few examples:

- *friend, wield, yield* (i before e)
- *receipt, deceive* (except after c)
- *weight, freight* (or when sounded as *a*)

Words Ending in *e*

Generally, the *e* at the end of English words is silent or not pronounced (e.g., *bake*).

- If the suffix being added to a root word begins with a consonant, keep the *e*.
- If the suffix begins with a vowel, the final silent *e* is dropped.

Root Word	Ending	Suffix	Spelling Change
waste	silent *e*	-ful	wasteful
remorse		-s	remorseful
pause			pauses
reserve	silent *e*	-ation	reservation
pause		-ing	pausing

Exceptions: When the root word ends in *ce* or *ge* and the suffix *–able* or *–ous* is being added, the silent final *e* is kept (e.g., *courageous, noticeable*).

Words Ending with *-ise* or *-ize*

Sometimes, it can be difficult to tell whether a word (usually a verb) should end in *–ise* or *–ize*. In American English, only a few words end with *–ise*. A few examples are *advertise, advise,* and *compromise*. Most words are more likely to end in *–ize*. A few examples are *accessorize, authorize, capitalize,* and *legalize*.

Words Ending with *-ceed, -sede,* or *-cede*

It can also be difficult to tell whether a word should end in *–ceed, –sede,* or *–cede*. In the English language, there are only three words that end with *–ceed*: *exceed, proceed,* and *succeed*. There is only one word that ends with *–sede*: *supersede*.

If a word other than *supersede* ends in a suffix that sounds like *–sede*, it should probably be *–cede*. For example: *concede, recede,* and *precede*.

Words Ending in *–able* or *–ible*

In the English language, more words end in *–able* than in *–ible*:

- e.g., *probable, actionable, approachable, traceable*
- e.g., *accessible, admissible, plausible*

Written Expression

Words Ending in -ance or -ence
The suffixes -ance and -ence are added to verbs to change them into nouns or adjectives that refer to a state of being. For example, when -ance is added to the verb perform, performance is formed, referring to the act of performing.

Suffix	When to use	Example
-ance, -ancy, -ant	• When the root word ends in a c that sounds like k • When the root word ends in a hard g	• significance • arrogance • vacancy • extravagant
-ence, -ency, -ent	• When the root word ends in a c that sounds like s • When the root word ends in a g that sounds like j	• adolescence • convergence • contingency • convergent

Words Ending in -tion, -sion, or -cian
The suffixes –tion and –sion are used when forming nouns that refer to the result of a verb. For example, the result of to abbreviate something is an abbreviation. Likewise, if a person has compressed something, then there is a compression.

The suffix –cian is used when referring to a person who practices something specific. For example, the person who practices politics is a politician.

Words Containing -ai or -ia
Unfortunately, there isn't an easy-to-remember rhyme for deciding whether a word containing the vowels a and i should be spelled ai or ia. In this case, it's helpful to rely on pronunciation to determine the correct spelling.

The combination of ai is one sound, as in the words captain and faint.

The combination of ia, on the other hand, is two separate sounds, as in the words guardian and diabolical.

It's helpful to say the word out loud to decide which combination of the two vowels is correct.

Rules for Plural Nouns

Nouns Ending in -ch, -sh, -s, -x, or -z
When modifying a noun that ends in ch, sh, s, x, or z to its plural form, add es instead of the singular s. For example, trench becomes trenches, ash becomes ashes, business becomes businesses, jukebox becomes jukeboxes, and fox becomes foxes.

This rule also applies to family names. For example, the Finch family becomes the Finches, and the Martinez family becomes the Martinezes.

Nouns Ending in *y* or *ay, ey, iy, oy,* or *uy*

When forming plurals with nouns ending in the consonant *y*, the *y* is replaced with *-ies*. For example, *spy* becomes *spies*, and *city* becomes *cities*.

If a noun ends with a vowel before a *y*, the *y* is kept, and an *s* is added. For example, *key* becomes *keys*, and *foray* becomes *forays*.

Nouns Ending in *f* or *fe*

When forming plurals with nouns ending in *f* or *fe*, the *f* is replaced with *v*, and *es* is added. For example, *half* becomes *halves*, and *knife* becomes *knives*.

Some exceptions are *roof/roofs* and *reef/reefs*.

Nouns Ending in *o*

When forming plurals with nouns ending in a consonant and *o*, the *o* is kept and an *es* is added. For example, *tomato* becomes *tomatoes*.

Musical terms are the exception to this rule. Words like *soprano* and *piano* are pluralized by adding *s* even though they end in a consonant and *o* (*sopranos, pianos*).

When forming plurals with nouns ending in a vowel and *o*, the *o* is kept, and *s* is added. For example, *ratio* becomes *ratios*, and *patio* becomes *patios*.

Exceptions to the Rules of Plurals

For some nouns, instead of changing or adding letters at the end of the word, changes to the vowels *within* the words are necessary. For example:

- *man* becomes *men*
- *woman* becomes *women*
- *child* becomes *children*

Some nouns, when pluralized, change entirely:

- *tooth* becomes *teeth*
- *foot* becomes *feet*
- *mouse* becomes *mice*

The opposite is also true; some nouns are the same in the plural as they are in the singular form. For example, *deer, species, fish,* and *sheep* are all plural nouns in singular form.

Clarity

In today's law enforcement world, the ability to write clearly and effectively is an important skill. Written communications such as incident reports and arrest reports are an integral part of the job, and being able to produce clear, comprehensive communications is essential.

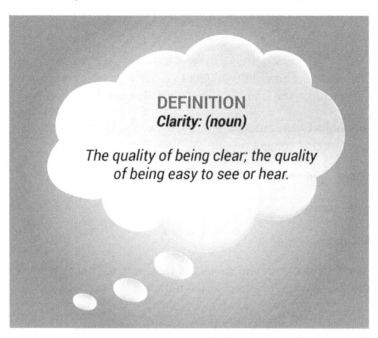

Clear written communication is important in everyday life—particularly in law enforcement. Officers are often responsible for creating a variety of daily reports, and writing content that's clear and concise results in more effective communications.

This section of the study guide focuses on writing *clarity*. The definition of clarity is "the quality of being clear." In writing, this means that the content is focused and the writer's intention is clear in both word choice and sentence structure. Why is this important? Writers want their readers to understand exactly what they're saying and NOT misinterpret their words. In the same sense, readers want a clear understanding of what they're reading. The following section covers understanding writing clarity through basic grammar principles.

Subjects and Predicates

Subjects
Every complete sentence is made up of two parts: a subject and a predicate. The **subject** is *who* or *what* the sentence is about. There are three subject types: simple, complete, and compound.

A **simple subject** tells *who* or *what* the sentence is about without additional details. For example:

> The blue car won the race.

In this sentence, the simple subject is the word *car*.

A **complete subject** contains the simple subject and its modifiers. In writing, a **modifier** is a word or phrase that gives more detail about a part of the sentence. In this case, the modifier gives more

information about the subject. When looking for a complete subject, first identify the verb or action word in the sentence (e.g., *run*, *jump*, *carried*), then ask to *who* or *what* the verb is referring. Look again at the previous example:

Sentence: The blue car won the race.

Identify the verb: *won*

Ask who or what won: *The blue car*

Answer: *The blue car* is the complete subject because it answers *what* won. Notice how the complete subject includes the simple subject (*car*) along with its modifier (*blue*).

If there's more than one subject in a sentence, it's called a **compound subject**. Look at the sentence below and identify the compound subject:

Sentence: John and I jumped over the huge puddle in the parking lot.

Identify the verb: *jumped*

Ask who or what jumped: *John and I*

Answer: *John and I* is the compound subject of the sentence because more than one subject can answer the question of *who* jumped over the puddle.

Predicates

In a sentence, the **predicate** usually tells something about the subject by describing what the subject does, is, or has. Similar to subjects, predicates are simple, complete, or compound.

A **simple predicate** is simply the verb. For example:

The dog ran into the busy road.

In this sentence, the simple predicate is the word *ran*.

A **complete predicate** contains the verb as well as its modifiers. In the example above, the complete predicate is *ran into the busy road*.

A **compound predicate** is when two or more words describe one subject. For example:

The flight was delayed and eventually canceled.

In this sentence, the compound predicate (*was delayed and eventually canceled*) provides two details about one subject (*The flight*).

Written Expression

Modeling Subjects and Predicates in a Sentence Diagram

A **sentence diagram** makes it easier to identify the subject and predicate in a sentence. To create one, draw a long horizontal line with a short vertical line going through it. Write the subject of the sentence to the left of the vertical line and the predicate to the right. Here's an example:

The black pen | ran out of ink on the last page of the document.

(*SUBJECT*)   (*PREDICATE*)

The vertical line divides the subject (*The black pen*) from the predicate (*ran out of ink*).

Subject-Verb Agreement

The basic rule of subject-verb agreement is that a **singular subject** (one person, place, or thing) requires a singular verb, while a **plural subject** (more than one person, place, or thing) needs a plural verb.

When a sentence is in the present tense and contains a singular subject, the singular verb usually ends with the letter *s*. For example:

Riley stacks the books on the shelf.

Since the subject (*Riley*) is singular, the verb needs to be singular (*stacks*). If the subject is plural, the verb must also be plural:

Riley and Nate stack the books on the shelf.

In this sentence the subject is plural (*Riley and Nate*) so the verb must be plural (*stack*). Subjects can be nouns (as above) or pronouns. When the subject is a singular pronoun such as *I* or *you*, the verb is also singular. In the case of *I* or *you*, though the verb is singular, it usually will not have an *s* on the end. For example:

Can *you call* for the pizza in ten minutes?

In this case the subject (*you*) is singular, so the verb (*call*) is also singular.

Subjects and verbs must also agree in point of view (POV) and verb tense (past, present, or future). The first-, second-, and third-person Point Of View pronouns (singular and plural) are shown below:

	First-Person POV	Second-Person POV	Third-Person POV
Singular Pronoun	I	You	He/She/It
Plural Pronoun	We	You	They

Using the chart above, look at the following examples of subject-verb agreement in relation to point of view and verb tense (in this case, present tense):

	Singular Verb	Plural Verb
First-Person POV	I am swimming.	We are swimming.
Second-Person POV	You are swimming.	You are swimming.
Third-Person POV	He is swimming.	They are swimming.

In each example above, the verb agrees with its singular or plural subject.

Words Between Subjects and Verbs

Interrupting words such as *of* and *to* are commonly used between subjects and verbs. For example:

> The lowest point *of* his career was yesterday, when he missed the penalty shot in the playoff game.

The subject here is *lowest point*, and the verb is *was*. Notice how the phrase *of his career* doesn't influence the verb *was*.

Compound Subjects

With a compound subject there's more than one subject (plural), so the verb must be plural. For example:

> *Mike and Vince* play basketball on Friday nights.

Notice how the compound subject (*Mike and Vince*) requires a plural verb (*play*) to agree.

Subjects Joined by *Or* or *Nor*

Singular subjects need a singular verb if they are joined by the words *or* or *nor*. If there are plural subjects, *the subject closest to the verb* determines if the verb is singular or plural. Here are examples of both:

> The table or the couch arrives tomorrow.

The singular verb (*arrives*) is used because the two singular subjects (*table* and *couch*) are joined by the word *or*.

> The table or the *couches* arrive tomorrow.

In this case, the plural verb (*arrive*) is used because the subject closest to the verb (*couches*) is plural.

Indefinite Pronouns *Either, Neither,* and *Each*

In a sentence, the words *either*, *neither*, and *each* act as singular subjects. For example:

> *Neither* of the printers *is* working properly.

Since the word *neither* acts as a singular subject, the verb (*is*) must also be singular.

The Adjectives *Every* and *Any* with Compounds

If a compound word contains the adjectives *every* and *any*, it acts as a singular subject, therefore making the verb singular. For example:

> *Everyone is* here for the surprise party!

Notice how the verb (*is*) is singular because the word *everyone* begins with *every*.

Written Expression

Collective Nouns

Collective nouns represent a group or collection of people, places, or things. Words such as *team*, *class*, *family*, and *jury* are all examples of collective nouns. When using a collective noun in a sentence, the verb is singular if the group is working together as a whole. For example:

Their *family is* waiting for the dog to come home.

The collective noun *family* determines the singular verb *is* instead of *are*. A simple trick would be to replace the collective noun with a pronoun. In this case, replace Their family with *it*, since *family* refers to a single unit.

Plural Form and Singular Meaning

Words such as *scissors*, *pants*, and *tweezers* are all examples of nouns that exist only in plural form. All are singular in meaning but plural in their structure. For plural nouns with singular meaning, the verb is singular. For example:

The *news is* doing a special on male teachers in elementary education.

Notice how *news* seems plural but is actually singular. Therefore, it uses the singular verb *is*.

Complements

Nouns, pronouns, and adjectives can act as **complements**, providing details to complete the meaning of a sentence. These so-called "sentence completers" include predicate nominatives, predicate adjectives, direct objects, and indirect objects. It's important to note that both predicate nominatives and predicate adjectives follow *linking verbs* (e.g., *is*, *am*, *are*, *was*, *were*, *be*, *being*, *been*) that show no action.

Predicate Nominatives

Predicate nominatives are nouns or pronouns that rename or modify the subject and *follow a linking verb*. For example:

My dog is a poodle.

In this sentence, the word *poodle* renames the subject (*dog*) and follows the linking verb (*is*).

Predicate Adjectives

Predicate adjectives are adjectives that rename or modify the subject and *follow a linking verb*. For example:

My cat is lazy.

In this sentence, the word *lazy* is the predicate adjective because it modifies the subject (*cat*) and follows the linking verb (*is*).

Direct Objects

A **direct object** is a noun, pronoun, or phrase that follows an action verb and answers the question *what* or *who* about the verb. Though a sentence needs a subject and a verb to be complete, it doesn't always need a direct object. To find the direct object in a sentence, look at the following formula:

Subject + Verb + *what*? or *who*? = Direct Object

Now, apply this formula to the following sentence:

    Spike and Sheena chased the ball around the house.

    Subject(s): *Spike and Sheena*

    Verb: *chased*

    Direct Object: *the ball*

Indirect Objects

An **indirect object** is a noun or pronoun that tells *to whom* or *for whom* the action of the verb is being done. A sentence must have a direct object to have an indirect object. When looking for the indirect object in a sentence, first find the verb and then ask the question *to whom* or *for whom*. For example:

    Lucy passed the crayon to her friend.

In this sentence, the indirect object is *her friend* because it answers *to whom* Lucy *passed* (verb) *the crayon* (direct object).

Pronoun Usage

A **pronoun** is a word that takes the place of a noun. This section looks at the different ways that pronouns are used in sentences.

Pronoun-Antecedent Agreement

An **antecedent** is a word or phrase that typically comes first, followed by a pronoun that refers to it. The pronoun must agree with its antecedent in form (singular or plural). For example:

    Singular Agreement:

        The *package* was dropped off at my door, and *it* was very heavy.

Here the antecedent (*package*) is singular, so the pronoun (*it*) must also be singular.

    Plural Agreement:

        The *packages* were dropped off at my door, and *they* were very heavy.

In this example, the antecedent (*packages*) is plural, so the pronoun (*they*) must also be in plural form.

When there are **compound subjects** (more than one subject) in a sentence, test each pronoun individually with the verb to determine which one is correct. To do this, simply remove the first subject, read the sentence with the remaining pronoun, and decide which one sounds better. For example, look at these two sentences:

    Mom and I are going to the park.

    Mom and me are going to the park.

Written Expression

Delete the first subject (*Mom*) from the sentences and then read them both (*I am going to the park* and *me is going to the park*). Which one sounds better? Clearly the first sentence, so the pronoun *I* is the correct choice.

Pronoun Reference

A pronoun shouldn't confuse the reader about whom or what it's describing, and it should clearly refer to its antecedent. For example:

Unclear: The shovel and the pail floated away in the ocean, and it was long gone.

In this sentence, it can't be determined if the pronoun *it* refers to *the shovel* or *the pail*.

Clear: The pail floated away in the ocean, and it was long gone.

In this sentence, the pronoun *it* clearly refers to its antecedent, *the pail*.

Personal Pronouns

Personal pronouns can be in the subjective, objective, or possessive case:

Subjective Case: The pronoun replaces the subject of the sentence.

Objective Case: The pronoun functions as the object.

Possessive Case: The pronoun shows possession of something.

The table below provides examples of each personal pronoun case:

Subjective	Objective	Possessive
I	Me	Mine
You	You	Yours
He	Him	His
She	Her	Hers
It	It	Its
We	Us	Ours
They	Them	Theirs
*Who	*Whom	Whose

*The pronouns *who* and *whom* are often used incorrectly. Use the pronoun *who* when referring to the *subject* of the sentence. Use the pronoun *whom* when referring to the *object* of the sentence.

In the following sentence, identify each pronoun and its case:

The flowers grew in his garden.

The pronoun is *his,* and it's in the possessive case.

Can someone please tell them to turn the music down?

The pronoun is *them,* and it's in the objective case.

Melissa is a really good cook, and she uses only fresh ingredients.

The pronoun is *she,* and it's in the subjective case.

Written Expression

Sentence Structures

There are many ways to organize the words in a sentence to clarify ideas. The four main sentence structures are simple sentences, compound sentences, complex sentences, and compound-complex sentences. In writing, using a variety of these structures makes the style more effective.

Simple Sentences
A **simple sentence** is made up of one independent clause. An **independent clause** is a separate complete thought that can stand on its own, and contains a subject and a predicate. Simple sentences can have compound subjects or compound verbs, but they can only have one main thought. The following is an example of a simple sentence:

> The bus was late.

The singular subject is *bus*, and the predicate is *was late*, so the sentence is a complete thought.

Compound Sentences
A **compound sentence** uses a conjunction to join two independent clauses. **Conjunctions** are linking words such as *and, but, for, nor, or, so,* and *yet*. For example:

> Bradley waited for the bus, but the bus was late.

In this sentence there are two complete thoughts (*Bradley waited for the bus* and *the bus was late*) joined by the conjunction *but*. Therefore, this is a compound sentence.

Complex Sentences
A **complex sentence** consists of one independent clause and one or more dependent clauses. A **dependent clause** is a clause that contains a subject and a verb, but can't stand on its own as a sentence. Complex sentences often use words like *after, although, before, while, wherever, if,* and *since*. For example:

> Although she really enjoyed the opera, Mary was very tired by the end of the night.

The first word in the sentence (*Although*) immediately attracts the reader's attention. The dependent clause (*Although she really enjoyed the opera*) is followed by the independent clause (*Mary was very tired by the end of the night*), which makes this a complex sentence.

Compound-Complex Sentences
A **compound-complex sentence** has at least two independent clauses and at least one dependent clause. For example:

> Although she really enjoyed the opera, Mary was very tired by the end of the night, and she still had to walk home.

The dependent clause (*Although she really enjoyed the opera*) depends on both the first independent clause (*Mary was very tired by the end of the night*) and the second independent clause (*and she still had to walk home*).

Sentence Fragments

A **sentence fragment** is an incomplete sentence that can't stand on its own. It's a dependent clause or phrase that looks like sentences but isn't. A sentence fragment may start with a capital letter and end with punctuation, but it isn't a complete thought. To revise a sentence fragment, either link the fragment to another sentence or add on to create a complete sentence. Look at the following example:

I turned off the television. Because the phone was ringing.

Fragment: *Because the phone was ringing.*

Possible revisions:

I turned off the television because the phone was ringing.

Because the phone was ringing, I ran upstairs to answer it.

Dangling and Misplaced Modifiers

Dangling Modifiers

A **dangling modifier** is a word or phrase where the word it's supposed to modify is missing. In other words, it has nothing to modify. It can also be a dependent clause that's not logically related to the word it should modify. To correct a dangling modifier, connect it to the word it's to modify. For example:

Dangling: Having designed the float for the parade, it will take six months to build it.

Revised: Having designed the float for the parade, he expects to build it in six months.

In the revision, *Having designed* now correctly modifies the subject of the sentence (*he*).

Misplaced Modifiers

A **misplaced modifier** is word or phrase that's separated from the word that it's supposed to modify. Though a modifier can be put in more than one place within a sentence, the modifier should be clearly attached to the word it describes. For example:

Misplaced: The dog almost chased the squirrel for an hour.

Revised: The dog chased the squirrel for almost an hour.

In this example, the dog didn't *almost* chase the squirrel, it *did* chase the squirrel. The revised version of the sentence connects the word *almost* to the words *an hour,* which creates the clearest meaning of the sentence.

Run-On Sentences

A **run-on sentence** has two or more independent clauses that aren't connected by any punctuation. Instead, the sentence goes on and on without any pauses or stops. Here are some ways to correct a run-on sentence:

Add a comma and a coordinating conjunction:

Incorrect: I loaded the dishwasher can you drain the sink?

Correct: I loaded the dishwasher, so can you drain the sink?

Add a semicolon, colon, or dash (without a coordinating conjunction) when the two independent clauses are related to each other:

Incorrect: I went to the movies at the snack bar I bought candy.

Correct: I went to the movies; there I bought candy at the snack bar.

Separate the clauses by turning them into two separate sentences:

Incorrect: The grocery store was busy it quickly sold out of bread.

Correct: The grocery store was busy. It quickly sold out of bread.

Turn one of the independent clauses into a phrase:

Incorrect: The grocery store was busy it quickly sold out of bread.

Correct: The busy grocery store quickly sold out of bread.

Vocabulary

Vocabulary is simply the words a person uses and understands on a daily basis. Having a good vocabulary is important in both written and verbal communications. In law enforcement, officers may have to read court records, police reports, and other legal documents. Many of these materials may contain unfamiliar words, so it's important for officers to learn ways to uncover a word's meaning so they can use it correctly in their own writing.

To understand the challenges of using vocabulary correctly, imagine suddenly being thrust into a foreign country. Not knowing the right words to use when asking for basic necessities (e.g., food, a place to stay, a bathroom) would make everyday life extremely difficult. Asking for help from foreigners who don't share the same vocabulary is hard, since language is what facilitates understanding between people. The more vocabulary words a person understands, the more precisely they can communicate their intentions. This section of the study guide focuses on understanding and deciphering vocabulary through basic grammar.

Prefixes and Suffixes

In the previous section, we went over the particular *spelling* of prefixes and suffixes, and how they changed the root word. In this section, we will look at the *meaning* of various prefixes and suffixes when

Written Expression

added to a root word. As mentioned before, a **prefix** is a combination of letters found at the beginning of a word, while a **suffix** is a combination of letters found at the end. A **root word** is the word that comes after the prefix, before the suffix, or between them both. Sometimes a root word can stand on its own without either a prefix or a suffix. More simply put:

Prefix + Root Word = Word

Root Word + Suffix = Word

Prefix + Root Word + Suffix = Word

Root Word = Word

Knowing the definitions of common prefixes and suffixes can help when trying to determine the meaning of an unknown word. In addition, knowing prefixes can help in determining the number of things, the negative of something, or the time and space of an object. Understanding suffix definitions can help when trying to determine the meaning of an adjective, noun, or verb.

The following charts review some of the most common prefixes, what they mean, and how they're used to decipher a word's meaning:

Number and Quantity Prefixes

Prefix	Definition	Example
bi-	two	bicycle, bilateral
mono-	one, single	monopoly, monotone
poly-	many	polygamy, polygon
semi-	half, partly	semiannual, semicircle
uni-	one	unicycle, universal

Here's an example of a number prefix:

The countries signed a *bilateral* agreement; both had to abide by the contract.

Look at the word *bilateral*. If the root word (*lateral*) is unfamiliar, the prefix (*bi-*) can provide a vital clue to its meaning. The prefix *bi-* means *two*, which shows that the agreement involves two of something, most likely the two countries, since *both had to abide by the contract*. This is correct since *bilateral* actually means "involving two parties, usually countries."

Negative Prefixes

Prefix	Definition	Example
a-	without, lack of	amoral, atypical
in-	not, opposing	inability, inverted
non-	not	nonexistent, nonstop
un-	not, reverse	unable, unspoken

Here's an example of a negative prefix:

> The patient's *inability* to speak made the doctor wonder what was wrong.

Look at the word *inability*. In the chart above, the prefix *in-* means *not* or *opposing*. By replacing the prefix with *not* and placing it in front of the root word of *ability* (*able*), the meaning of the word becomes clear: *not able*. Therefore, the patient was *not able* to speak.

Time and Space Prefixes

Prefix	Definition	Example
a-	in, on, of, up, to	aloof, associate
ab-	from, away, off	abstract, absent
ad-	to, towards	adept, adjacent
ante-	before, previous	antebellum, antenna
anti-	against, opposing	anticipate, antisocial
cata-	down, away, thoroughly	catacomb, catalogue
circum-	around	circumstance, circumvent
com-	with, together, very	combine, compel
contra-	against, opposing	contraband, contrast
de-	from	decrease, descend
dia-	through, across, apart	diagram, dialect
dis-	away, off, down, not	disregard, disrespect
epi-	upon	epidemic, epiphany
ex-	out	example, exit
hypo-	under, beneath	hypoallergenic, hypothermia
inter-	among, between	intermediate, international
intra-	within	intrapersonal, intravenous
ob-	against, opposing	obtain, obscure
per-	through	permanent, persist
peri-	around	periodontal, periphery
post-	after, following	postdate, postoperative
pre-	before, previous	precede, premeditate
pro-	forward, in place of	program, propel
retro-	back, backward	retroactive, retrofit
sub-	under, beneath	submarine, substantial
super-	above, extra	superior, supersede
trans-	across, beyond, or over	transform, transmit
ultra-	beyond, excessively	ultraclean, ultralight

Here's an example of a space prefix:

> The teacher's motivational speech helped *propel* her students toward greater academic achievement.

Look at the word *propel*. The prefix *pro-* means *forward* or *in place of* which indicates something relevant to time and space. *Propel* means to drive or move in a direction (usually forward), so knowing the prefix *pro-* helps interpret that the students are moving forward *toward greater academic achievement*.

Miscellaneous Prefixes

Prefix	Definition	Example
belli-	war, warlike	bellied, belligerent
bene-	well, good	benediction, beneficial
equi-	equal	equidistant, equinox
for-	away, off, from	forbidden, forsaken
fore-	previous	forecast, forebode
homo-	same, equal	homogeneous, homonym
hyper-	excessive, over	hyperextend, hyperactive
in-	in, into	insignificant, invasive
magn-	large	magnetic, magnificent
mal-	bad, poorly, not	maladapted, malnourished
mis-	bad, poorly, not	misplace, misguide
mor-	death	mortal, morgue
neo-	new	neoclassical, neonatal
omni-	all, everywhere	omnipotent, omnipresent
ortho-	right, straight	orthodontist, orthopedic
over-	above	overload, overstock,
pan-	all, entire	panacea, pander
para-	beside, beyond	paradigm, parameter
phil-	love, like	philanthropy, philosophic
prim-	first, early	primal, primer
re-	backward, again	reload, regress
sym-	with, together	symmetry, symbolize
vis-	to see	visual, visibility

Here's another prefix example:

The computer was *primitive*; it still had a floppy disk drive!

The word *primitive* has the prefix *prim-* which indicates being *first* or *early*. *Primitive* means the historical development of something. Therefore, the sentence infers that the computer is an older model because it no longer has a floppy disk drive.

The charts that follow review some of the most common suffixes and include examples of how they're used to determine the meaning of a word. Remember, suffixes are added to the *end* of a root word:

Adjective Suffixes

Suffix	Definition	Example
-able (-ible)	capable of being	teachable, accessible
-esque	in the style of, like	humoresque, statuesque
-ful	filled with, marked by	helpful, deceitful
-ic	having, containing	manic, elastic
-ish	suggesting, like	malnourish, tarnish
-less	lacking, without	worthless, fearless
-ous	marked by, given to	generous, previous

Here's an example of an adjective suffix:

The live model looked so *statuesque* in the window display; she didn't even move!

Look at the word *statuesque*. The suffix *-esque* means *in the style of* or *like*. If something is *statuesque*, it's *in the style of a statue* or *like a statue*. In this sentence, the model looks *like* a statue.

Noun Suffixes

Suffix	Definition	Example
-acy	state, condition	literacy, legacy
-ance	act, condition, fact	distance, importance
-ard	one that does	leotard, billiard
-ation	action, state, result	legislation, condemnation
-dom	state, rank, condition	freedom, kingdom
-er (-or)	office, action	commuter, spectator
-ess	feminine	caress, princess
-hood	state, condition	childhood, livelihood
-ion	action, result, state	communion, position
-ism	act, manner, doctrine	capitalism, patriotism
-ist	worker, follower	stylist, activist
-ity (-ty)	state, quality, condition	community, dirty
-ment	result, action	empowerment, segment
-ness	quality, state	fitness, rudeness
-ship	position	censorship, leadership
-sion (-tion)	state, result	tension, transition
-th	act, state, quality	twentieth, wealth
-tude	quality, state, result	attitude, latitude

Look at the following example of a noun suffix:

The *spectator* cheered when his favorite soccer team scored a goal.

Look at the word *spectator*. The suffix *-or* means *action*. In this sentence, the *action* is to *spectate* (watch something), thus a *spectator* is someone involved in watching something.

Written Expression

Verb Suffixes

Suffix	Definition	Example
-ate	having, showing	facilitate, integrate
-en	cause to be, become	frozen, written
-fy	make, cause to have	modify, rectify
-ize	cause to be, treat with	realize, sanitize

Here's an example of a verb suffix:

The preschool had to *sanitize* the toys every Tuesday and Thursday.

In the word *sanitize*, the suffix *-ize* means *cause to be* or *treat with*. By adding the suffix *-ize* to the root word *sanitary*, the meaning of the word becomes active: *cause to be sanitary*.

Context Clues

It's common to encounter unfamiliar words in written communication. When faced with an unknown word, there are certain "tricks" that can be used to uncover its meaning. **Context clues** are words or phrases within a sentence or paragraph that provide hints about a word and its definition. For example, if an unfamiliar word is anchored to a noun with other attached words as clues, these can help decipher the word's meaning. Consider the following example:

After the treatment, Grandma's natural rosy cheeks looked *wan* and ghostlike.

The unfamiliar word is *wan*. The first clue to its meaning is in the phrase *After the treatment,* which implies that something happened after a procedure (possibly medical). A second clue is the word *rosy*, which describes Grandma's natural cheek color that changed after the treatment. Finally, the word *ghostlike* infers that Grandma's cheeks now look white. By using the context clues in the sentence, the meaning of the word *wan* (which means *pale*) can be deciphered.

Below are some additional ways to use context clues to uncover the meaning of an unknown word:

Contrasts
Look for context clues that *contrast* the unknown word. When reading a sentence with an unfamiliar word, look for a contrasting or opposing word or idea. Here's an example:

Since Mary didn't cite her research sources, she lost significant points for *plagiarizing* the content of her report.

In this sentence, **plagiarizing** is the unfamiliar word. Notice that when Mary *didn't cite her research sources,* it resulted in her losing points for *plagiarizing the content of her report*. These contrasting ideas infer that Mary did something wrong with the content. This makes sense because the definition of *plagiarizing* is "taking the work of someone else and passing it off as your own."

Contrasts often use words like *but, however, although,* or phrases like *on the other hand*. For example:

The *gargantuan* television won't fit in my car, but it will cover the entire wall in the den.

The unfamiliar word is *gargantuan*. Notice that the television is too big to fit in a car, <u>*but it will cover the entire wall in the den*</u>. This infers that the television is extremely large, which is correct, since the word *gargantuan* means "enormous."

Synonyms

Another method is to brainstorm possible synonyms for the unknown word. **Synonyms** are words with the same or similar meanings (e.g., *strong* and *sturdy*). To do this, substitute synonyms one at a time, reading the sentence after each to see if the meaning is clear. By replacing an unknown word with a known one, it may be possible to uncover its meaning. For example:

> Gary's clothes were *saturated* after he fell into the swimming pool.

In this sentence, the word *saturated* is unknown. To brainstorm synonyms for *saturated*, think about what happens to Gary's clothes after falling into the swimming pool. They'd be *soaked* or *wet*, both of which turn out to be good synonyms to try since the actual meaning of *saturated* is "thoroughly soaked."

Antonyms

Sometimes sentences contain words or phrases that oppose each other. Opposite words are known as **antonyms** (e.g., *hot* and *cold*). For example:

> Although Mark seemed *tranquil*, you could tell he was actually nervous as he paced up and down the hall.

The unknown word here is *tranquil*. The sentence says that Mark was in fact not *tranquil* but was instead *actually nervous*. The opposite of the word *nervous* is *calm*, which is the meaning of the word *tranquil*.

Explanations or Descriptions

Explanations or descriptions of other things in the sentence can also provide clues to an unfamiliar word. Take the following example:

> Golden Retrievers, Great Danes, and Pugs are the top three *breeds* competing in the dog show.

If the word *breeds* is unknown, look at the sentence for an explanation or description that provides a clue. The subjects (*Golden Retrievers*, *Great Danes*, and *Pugs*) describe different types of dogs. This description helps uncover the meaning of the word *breeds* which is "a particular type or group of animals."

Inferences

Sometimes there are clues to an unknown word that infer or suggest its meaning. These **inferences** can be found either within the sentence where the word appears or in a sentence that precedes or follows it. Look at the following example:

> The *wretched* old lady was kicked out of the restaurant. She was so mean and nasty to the waiter!

Here the word *wretched* is unknown. The first sentence states that the *old lady was kicked out of the restaurant*, but it doesn't say why. The sentence that follows tells us why: *She was so mean and nasty to*

Written Expression

the waiter! This infers that the old lady was *kicked out* because she was *so mean and nasty* or, in other words, *wretched*.

When preparing for a vocabulary test, try reading challenging materials to learn new words. If a word on the test is unfamiliar, look for prefixes and suffixes to help uncover what the word means and eliminate incorrect answers. If two answers both seem right, determine if there are any differences between them and then select the word that best fits. Context clues in the sentence or paragraph can also help to uncover the meaning of an unknown word. By learning new vocabulary words, a person can expand their knowledge base and improve the quality and effectiveness of their written communications.

Practice Quiz

For the first three questions, choose the word that is spelled correctly.

1. I'm _____ looking forward to my vacation this year.
    a. definitly
    b. definitely
    c. defenitely
    d. definately

2. I hope that scientists are able to prove the _____ of aliens.
    a. existanse
    b. esixtinse
    c. existense
    d. existence

3. _____ speaking, our operating system is one of the best on the market.
    a. Technicaly
    b. Technicilly
    c. Technically
    d. Technikcally

For the next two questions, choose the synonym for the underlined word.

4. The city's first responders must follow <u>protocol</u> when handling calls for cases of domestic violence.
    a. Guidelines
    b. Internist
    c. Requests
    d. Evidence

5. After the riot broke out, officers had to use strong measures to <u>quell</u> the angry crowd.
    a. Wave
    b. Count
    c. Incite
    d. Calm

See answers on next page.

Answer Explanations

1. **B:** definitely

2. **D:** existence

3. **C:** Technically

4. **A:** *Guidelines* and *protocol* can be used as synonyms.

Guidelines: a set of standards created for a future action

Protocol: official guidelines or procedures that must be followed

5. **D:** *Calm* and *quell* can be used as synonyms.

Calm: to make tranquil or serene

Quell: to calm, quiet, or put an end to something

Memorization

Memorization

The Memory section assesses a candidate's observational skills and his or her ability to recall facts and information. This is a very important skill that officers must employ daily during routine job duties.

On the exam, this section is typically composed of a couple of drawings or photographs that are followed by a series of multiple-choice questions. The questions are not viewable until the image is removed. Test takers examine each graphic one at a time, and then the image is removed. During the observation period, it is recommended that test takers study the image as carefully as possible, first examining the overall scene and then studying it more closely to identify and memorize details.

The questions that follow pertain to details from the graphic and must be completed from memory. Access to review the image again is not permitted. Because the questions pertaining to the image may address the picture on a general level as well as specific details, both elements need to be examined. For example, test takers may encounter an image of a prison cell containing several inmates who are fighting. One question may address the image as a whole, such as: "*what is the general mood of the image?*" Answer choices may be options such as *triumphant, hopeful, agitated*, and *peaceful.* In this case, *agitated* is the best choice. The majority of the questions will be about more specific details from the image. For example, questions for this same image may ask how many inmates were present in the scene, what time was displayed on the wall clock, what was the position of the cell door, or how many bars were running vertically on the window.

There are a variety of strategies that candidates employ to improve their scores in this section. Most test takers start by examining the entire image for a few seconds and then moving from this broad view to an increasingly specific study. Some people find that it works best to examine the picture in quadrants or in designated sections individually in a predetermined order to ensure that the entire image is studied without leaving gaps. Other candidates employ a variety of strategies depending on the particular image. For example, they may study the people first and then the environment surrounding the scene for an outdoor picture or start by looking at the walls and then the middle of the room indoors.

Other test takers start by trying to identify context clues from the scene, such as the sun position or weather in outdoor scenes or the clock time indoors to determine the season or time of day. Then, they may move on to try to count specific figures or subjects in the scene and identify distinguishing characteristics between such figures. For example, are there a different number of males and females present? Is someone wearing a distinguishing piece of clothing such as a hat? Exam questions often address things such as the time, place, and setting of the graphic. Others ask test takers to recall the number of certain items present, or to answer questions about a specific item in the image, which can be better answered if distinguishing features of the items are noted during the study period.

It is recommended that test takers practice with a variety of images and strategies to familiarize themselves with the process and to identify those methods that work best. A sample graphic similar to those that may be encountered on the exam is provided below. Test takers should study the graphic for two minutes and then completely remove it from their view while attempting the practice questions. Test takers can practice this section an unlimited number of times with the help of a partner or friend. The partner can find any type of image and generate a few questions about it and then pass it to the test candidate to attempt.

Interpreting Visual Depictions of Traffic Incidents

In cases in which traffic patterns are involved, it is important for an officer to be able to identify where traffic incidents have occurred. Different visual representations may be used online and physically to depict these situations. An officer needs to be able to interpret this data in its different forms in order to decide where the event occurred and the best course of action to take.

It is important to look for descriptions that detail how the visual data is represented for a given traffic incident depiction. The officer should look for areas of the depiction where symbols are described or defined as well as instructional text that may detail how the information is to be interpreted. Then, once the layout of the data is clear to the officer, the visual depiction can be scanned to locate the traffic incident and the surrounding area. Different visual depictions may need to be used to identify a specific problem. In this case, the officer should look for the information that relates to the incident and gather all the data needed to completely understand the situation and be up to date on any recent changes in traffic patterns.

Recognizing and Identifying Facial Features

Being an officer requires keen observational skills and careful attention to detail to identify and interpret important information when it comes to solving a case. In the instance of identifying potential culprits, the officer will need to pay close attention to the features of individuals who may be involved in the incident. Sketch artists help officers by rendering images of suspects based on spoken, visual descriptions. They will then create a sketch of what the person potentially looks like, making sure the sketch is as accurate as possible so that it is identifiable to others. However, an officer will often still have to look through numerous sketches to identify a specific person. To be able to accomplish this task and pick the most accurate drawing, the officer needs to have a strong memory of the individual particulars that make up the person they are matching with the sketch.

When identifying facial features, an officer should focus on specific details that stand out. Things that may appear more pronounced in the individual than on other faces should be taken note of as well as body modifications such as tattoos and piercings. These will help distinguish the individual from others when asked to identify them later on. However, trying to keep track of too much information may be confusing when it comes time to recall a specific face; therefore, to be sure their memory is correct, an officer should focus on the details that are the easiest to remember. They should also keep in mind that drawings will never be exact and they are searching only for the closest similarity, not the one that perfectly matches the face remembered. If an officer is having trouble recalling features or is stuck between similar options, the best choice will be the one with the most specific remembered features to match any verbal descriptions that may have been used to describe the individual to the artist.

Visualizing and Identifying Patterns and Objects

To compile the most resources available to an officer for solving cases, large amounts of data need to be collected and recorded. It will be the officer's job to interpret this data to reach accurate conclusions, turning scattered information into a more coherent case that can be visualized and interpreted. A lot of sensory data will need to be kept track of and deciphered to give the most objective description of an incident. Visual data will need to be recalled in order for situations to be recreated and utilized. The best way to organize this visual data when recalling an incident is to identify patterns and specific objects.

Important information in a case will often be repeated in different ways by different people. Identifying correlating data will help determine the veracity of the information because it can be confirmed by multiple sources and noted as patterns. For example, multiple witnesses may give different information about how tall a suspect may be but each mention that the suspect had a more noticeable trait such as long hair. Another example is if each party involved agrees to the time of a car accident. When the officer starts gaining additional information and identifying more patterns that are important objects involved in a case, they can better visualize the instance to help determine the best course of action to take. Visualizations of events help an officer organize and structure an incident to examine all possible conclusions.

Recalling Information from Wanted Posters

Wanted posters are used to relay information about individuals involved in open cases. It is important for an officer to familiarize themselves with different types of wanted posters so they can identify important information that may need to be recalled later to solve a case. The more information the officer is able to take mental note of, the better equipped they will be to find and identify a wanted person. It is unreasonable to assume that all the information written on a wanted poster will be memorized by an officer, especially if multiple wanted posters are involved; however, an officer is expected to know enough about the case to recall the key details needed when the wanted poster is not available.

To know what information is the most significant to focus on, it is first important to identify how the information on the wanted poster is laid out. Most people may think of the Old West when they think about wanted posters, with bold letters identifying the criminal and the crimes committed as well as a large picture of the wanted person in the center. Wanted posters as they appear now are actually relatively unchanged from what they used to be, formatted in the same way to convey the most important information as quickly as possible.

First, the officer should study the face of the individual on the poster enough to be able to recall it and then take note of the specific information, such as height, weight, and eye color, to be able to form and visualize an image of the way the complete person may appear. Once the officer is able to form a mental picture of the culprit based on the image and the description, they can then focus on the specific crimes committed in order to relate the facts of the case; these can usually be found in a text-based description surrounding the photo. Once a few of the most specific details are memorized, the officer can go to the next wanted poster and repeat the process until they can recall each individual in their mind without referring to the posters.

Memorization

Ordering and Managing Facts Logically

Details for a case can build up quickly as new information comes in from different sources. Multiple people will also usually be involved in a case, making it important for an officer to be able to order and manage the facts from multiple accounts of an incident to reach the most informed conclusions. Data that has not been logically ordered is difficult to understand and may lead to confusion and an inability to find the true facts of a case. When the information is organized and presented in a way that is easier to follow, solutions to the problems are more identifiable because all the relevant details can be processed in a logical progression. When a case is just beginning, information will come to the officer in a disorganized way; it will be up to the officer to find all the facts of the case and reorganize them so they can be better used and understood. It is also important to have this logical progression of facts in order for others who may not have collected the data to be able to read about and understand the case at any moment.

Common instances of scrambled facts come in the form of witness statements. Several factors, such as the high emotional states of the witnesses, their lack of factual details, or the sheer number of witnesses involved, contribute to the sometimes disorganized data an officer receives. When obtaining information from a witness, an officer needs to first identify the facts of the case. True facts can be validated from multiple sources; they also are spoken with more confidence and relate to specific, objective details over emotional experiences. Once the officer has identified all the facts in an incident, they can then begin to place the facts in logical order. It is helpful for the officer to progress in a linear way, starting with what happened first and providing a progression of events up until the time of reporting. Once the facts follow a forward trajectory, they can be better used to recreate the scene and progress the information into a conclusion.

Finding the Perpetrator from a Description

When someone is arrested, information about their appearance and the crime or crimes they are being accused of is recorded. If the suspect in a case is still unknown, officers will most likely arrest multiple people. It is then the officer's job to determine which suspect is the culprit based on descriptions and information about those who have been arrested. Information provided to the officer may be in the form of a sketch or image, but often an officer will have to interpret written or spoken words used to describe the perpetrator. The officer will need to know how to best use this information to form an image of what the perpetrator may look like and to choose the corresponding person from a group of arrested suspects.

When processing information about an arrested person, the officer needs to first identify the key details that describe how the perpetrator may look. It is important to focus on descriptions that are unique and, if possible, character defining, that may help single the individual out from a group of similar-looking individuals. An officer should be careful of general descriptions, such as "tall" or "old," that are imprecise and can be relative to the individual who gave the information and focus on descriptions that can be easily visually recognizable. The officer should be able to form a detailed mental image of what they believe the culprit looks like based on the descriptions given. Then, when presented with those arrested, the officer can use this mental image to match which person they believe to be the perpetrator. However, an officer should never guess; if no arrests match the descriptions or lack distinctive details given about the perpetrator, more information will need to be gathered before a final decision should be made.

Identifying Meaningful Details

A scenario can involve a web of different and often conflicting sets of details. It is important for an officer to be able to identify the most and least meaningful details of a police scenario in order to focus on the information that will be the most helpful to solving a case. Although it is important to take note of as many details as possible when first encountering a case, in the long run, too many details for a given scenario will cause confusion if they are not vetted and organized. Focusing on finding the most and least meaningful details divides the information into what is the most relevant to the situation and what is superfluous to the case as a whole.

To discover which details are the most meaningful, it is important to first focus on the objective facts of the case. An officer should determine the beginning, middle, and end of the event; look for details that can be verified, such as time of day or objects involved; and value the information that is the most irrefutable, such as pictures or video of a scene. The credibility of each source should also be researched; the most credible information will be free from frequent changes of thought or details and will be the most understandable or logical in relation to the scenario.

The most meaningful details will also be frequently repeated, appearing in more than one source. The officer should determine what the frame of mind may have been like for those involved and how that might affect the information they have given. The least meaningful details in a police scenario will be the lies. It is important for the officer to spot where the untruthful information is and identify why it does not correlate with other data examined. Details that have no relation to the people or objects involved in the case are not very meaningful and should be set aside when organizing data into a complete case, whereas the most important details should be made to stand out.

Filling in Police Forms

Police forms are used by officers to organize information in a set way that can be easily interpreted by anyone who comes into contact with the information. This is done to set a standard behind all information reported for consistency of documentation. Forms will contain details related to an incident and will be used as a way to relay information about a case internally between parties. A police officer needs to be familiar with what these forms look like and the protocol for filling in blank reports or answering questions from a filled-in form. This way, they are able to not only file their own forms but to read and interpret the forms filled out by another officer.

Most information regarding an incident that is not directly witnessed will come to an officer in the form of a written incident description. It will then be the officer's job to use this written description to fill out a blank police department form. The form will help lay the information out in a way that others in the police department have been trained to interpret. There will be separate sections pertaining to different details of an event or crime. An officer should look at the headings of the forms to determine what information to provide for each section, being as detailed as possible without providing too much unimportant information.

The written description should not simply be copied over to the police form. The officer will need to interpret which data is the most important and how this data can be used to solve the case. Then, the officer will have to be able to read these forms to answer questions about an incident. Details should be able to be quickly spotted with the form because they will be laid out in a familiar way. Once the officer has familiarized themselves with the layout of the form, they can easily go to the specific section that contains the data needed to answer a question.

Practice Image

Directions:

Examine the image below for two minutes then remove it from view. Answer the questions that follow the image without referring back to the image. Do not read the questions during the image review period.

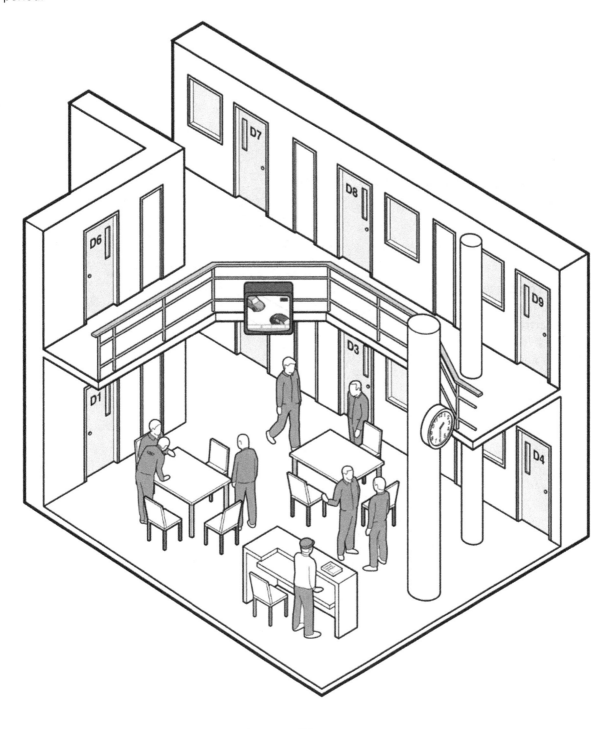

Memorization

1. How many doors are located on the second floor?
    a. 1
    b. 2
    c. 3
    d. 4

2. How many inmates are located at the table on the left?
    a. 3
    b. 4
    c. 5
    d. 6

3. What time is it?
    a. 7:50
    b. 2:30
    c. 12:10
    d. 4:00

4. What is written on the right most door downstairs?
    a. D4
    b. D9
    c. C9
    d. C4

5. What was on the television?
    a. Animals
    b. A cartoon
    c. Cars
    d. The news

See answers on next page.

Answers

1. D
2. A
3. B
4. A
5. C

Reasoning

Inductive and Deductive Reasoning

Generally speaking, there are two main types of reasoning—deductive and inductive. An inference based on **deductive reasoning** considers a principle that is generally believed to be true and then applies it to a specific situation ("All English majors love reading. Annabelle is an English major. Therefore, I can infer that Annabelle loves reading."). **Inductive reasoning** makes an inference by using specific evidence to make a general inference ("Trina, Arnold, and Uchenna are all from Florida. Trina, Arnold, and Uchenna all love to swim. Therefore, I can infer that people from Florida usually love swimming."). Both deductive and inductive reasoning use what is *known* to be true to make a logical guess about what is *probably* true.

As readers are presented with new information, they should organize it, make sense of it, and reflect on what they learned from the text. Readers draw conclusions at the end of a text by bringing together all of the details, descriptions, facts, and/or opinions presented by the author and asking, "What did I gain from reading this text? How have my ideas or emotions changed? What was the author's overall purpose for writing?" In this case, a **conclusion** is a unifying idea or final thought about the text that the reader can form after they are done reading. As discussed, sometimes writers are very explicit in stating what conclusions should be drawn from a text and what readers are meant to have learned. However, more often than not, writers simply present descriptions or information and then leave it up to readers to draw their own conclusions. As with making inferences, though, readers always need to base their conclusions on textual evidence rather than simply guessing or making random statements.

> When the school district's uniform policy was first introduced fifteen years ago, parents and students alike were incredibly enthusiastic about it. Some of the most appealing arguments in favor of enforcing school uniforms was to create an equal learning environment for all students, to eliminate the focus on fashion and appearance, and to simplify students' morning routine by removing the need to pick a different outfit every day. However, despite this promising beginning, the uniform policy has steadily lost favor over the years. First of all, schools did not notice a significant drop in examples of bullying at school, and students continue to report that they feel judged on their appearance based on things like weight and hairstyle. This seems to indicate that uniforms have not been particularly effective at removing the social pressure that teens feel to appear a certain way in front of their peers. Also, many parents have complained that the school's required uniform pieces like jackets, sweaters, and neckties can only be purchased from one specific clothing shop. Because this retailer has cornered the market on school uniforms, they are operating under a total monopoly, and disgruntled parents feel that they are being grossly overcharged for school clothing for their children. The uniform policy is set to be debated at the upcoming school board meeting, and many expect it to be overturned.

After reading this article, a reader might conclude any of the following: that ideas that start with popular support might become unpopular over time; or that there are several compelling counterarguments to the benefits of school uniforms; or that this school district is open to new ideas but also open to criticism. While each conclusion is slightly different, they are all based on information and evidence from the article, and therefore all are plausible. Each conclusion sums up what the reader learned from the passage and what overall idea the writer seems to be communicating.

Another way for readers to make sense of information in a text is to make **generalizations**. This is somewhat related to the concept of inductive reasoning, by which readers move from specific evidence to a more general idea. When readers generalize, they take the specific content of a text and apply it to a larger context or to a different situation. Let's make a generalization from the topic, the bystander effect:

> A bystander is simply a person who watches something happen. Paradoxically, the more people who witness an accident happen, the less likely each individual is to actually intervene and offer assistance. This is known as the bystander effect. Psychologists attribute the bystander effect to something called "diffusion of responsibility." If one individual witnesses an accident, that single person feels the whole burden of responsibility to respond to the accident. However, if there are many witnesses, each person feels that responsibility has been divided amongst many people, so their individual sense of responsibility is much lower and they are less likely to offer help.

This article describes one very specific psychological phenomenon known as the "bystander effect." However, based on this specific information, a reader could form a more general psychological statement such as, "Humans sometimes behave differently when they are alone and when they are in a group."

Applying Police Policies

It is important for an officer to completely understand the written details of any case they may be working on. Police policies have been put in place to create a method for examining and interpreting data presented to an officer. When an officer applies these police policies, they have a better chance of completely comprehending the case and can make better use of the data presented. Having the most important details is not enough if the officer cannot understand and use these details to make the most informed decisions. An officer should read all the details of an incident to have a clear understanding of each case that is presented to them. Although there may not be an objectively right way to interpret data, when it comes to the law, the most accurate interpretation will be the one that most coincides with the written law. Police policies are the tools an officer will use to interpret information by this standard of the law.

To start applying police policies to given situations, an officer needs to have a clear understanding of the policies of their local office. The officer should study the law definitions and be able to relate incidents to specific crimes as they are defined in text. Having a clear understanding of the laws in their area is the first step to applying these policies to specific cases. Once a thorough understanding of the law has been established, an officer should read and reread each report of an incident brought to them until they can form as clear a picture of the scene as possible. Then, the officer can start to draw comparisons to what they have read about the law, and specific police policies can be applied to the situation.

Frequency of Information Questions

Some of the most useful information involved in a case will come directly from witnesses. However, not all witnesses will give completely accurate information that can be used to solve the crime. It will be up to the officer to determine what information is factual and which witnesses are giving the most accurate reports of the incident.

When determining which witness is giving the most factual details of a case, there are a few factors the officer can immediately determine, such as if the witness was actually there at the time of the crime or the amount of details a witness actually observed. If the witness was too far away to see anything important or if they were not directly involved in the case, their information will most likely not be worth much attention. An officer should also take into consideration how much time has passed between the crime and the questioning of the witness; if more time has elapsed, the information may not be remembered as clearly.

After the witness's relation to the scene of the crime is determined, the officer can then interpret the confidence and completeness of their responses to determine which is the most truthful. True statements will be made confidently and stated in a way that can be clearly understood. True information will also appear frequently in more than one witness's testimony. If details about a case are repeated in the same way by multiple witnesses, the officer knows the information is most likely true. The witness who is telling the truth will be the one who can be backed up by other sources of evidence as well. The officer should ask about key details they already know to be true to see how the witness responds. The witness who is the most truthful will be the one who can back up their story with factual data.

Reading Maps to Find the Quickest Route

An officer should be familiar with different types of visual maps so they can always know the quickest route to a specific location. Road maps, subway maps, traffic maps, bus routes, etc., should all be able to be read quickly regardless of the map's visual style. An officer will need to know how to use both online and physical maps and be able to direct themselves as well as others as to the best route to take at a given time.

Generally, the easiest way to interpret a map is to look for the map key. The key will contain all the information relating to what each symbol on the map means as well as the distance scale that determines how far areas are from each other. Some maps may have this information explained in text instead of in a separate key, so the officer will need to know where to find the information that explains how the map is to be used. Finding the quickest route then means knowing where the initial starting point is, analyzing the routes on the map, and identifying which route provides the shortest amount of travel time. It is important to remember that sometimes the shortest distance between two points is not the quickest route. Traffic patterns, stops, speed limits, or other restrictions could add more travel time depending on the route and should be taken into consideration when searching for the most efficient route.

Comparative Values

A **comparative value** item provides details about specific subjects, like types of fruit or family members, and then asks that comparisons be drawn between them. There are two possible tasks:

- Order the subjects from *least to greatest* or *greatest to least*
- Find *the value* of a certain subject

Reasoning

When encountering a comparative value item, it's helpful to make a list and fill it in according to information given in the prompt. Everything needed to answer this type of question correctly is in the question. Here's an example:

> A vehicle rental company stocks cars, vans, busses, and trucks. The company ranks their vehicles by popularity so that they know what to buy when expanding their business. Cars are ranked between vans and trucks. Trucks are more popular than vans. Buses are ranked lowest. Which type of vehicle is rented the most?
>
> a. Cars
> b. Vans
> c. Busses
> d. Trucks

C   V   T   B

The items being compared are the prompt's subjects. In this question, there are cars, vans, buses, and trucks. Assigning them a letter or an image, as illustrated above, is a helpful way to list them quickly. For this question, the first letter of each vehicle represents the subject: C (car), V (van), T (truck), and B (bus).

Note what the prompt actually asks. In this prompt, the goal is to find which vehicle is rented *the most*. Thus, the list needs to be ordered from *most to least*:

Vehicles Rented – Most to Least

Determine which information is stated outright, meaning it is known for sure. In this prompt, *buses are ranked the lowest,* so buses can be placed at the bottom of the list:

Vehicles Rented – Most to Least
B

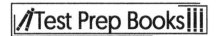

Next, look through the prompt for more information. This prompt states that *cars are ranked between vans and trucks*, so the list can look one of two ways:

Vehicles Rented – Most to Least *Possibility 1*	Vehicles Rented – Most to Least *Possibility 2*
V	T
C	C
T	V
B	B

To decide which list is correct, look for the last piece of information given in the prompt. In this prompt, *trucks are more popular than vans.* Which one of the lists shows that to be true?

Vehicles Rented – Most to Least
T
C
V
B

Revisit the final question to determine the response. *Which vehicle is being rented the most?* The answer is *D*, Trucks.

Numerical Series

A **numerical series** item presents a list of numbers and asks test takers to determine what the next number should be. The key to answering this type of question correctly is to understand *the relationship between the numbers* in the series. Do they increase or decrease, and at what rate? Is there a pattern? Here's an example:

Identify the next number in the series: 7, 14, 21, 28, 35, ...
 a. 42
 b. 28
 c. 47
 d. 50

First, decide if the numbers in the list are *increasing* or *decreasing*. Generally, if numbers increase, it is indicative of addition or multiplication. If they decrease, subtraction or division is more likely.

The numbers in this list are *increasing*: 7, 14, 21, 28, 35.

Here's a strategy to determine *the rate* at which they are increasing:

7,   14,   21,   28,   35

   +7   +7   +7   +7

Reasoning

The numbers in the list are increasing by 7. The rate of increase is constant throughout the list. Note that not all lists will increase or decrease at a constant rate.

To find the answer to this question, simply continue the rate of increase by adding 7 to 35. The answer is A, 42.

Here's a more complicated example:

Identify the next number in the series: 2, 3, 5, 9, 17...
a. 24
b. 33
c. 37
d. 39

Again, the first thing to do is decide if the numbers in the list are increasing or decreasing. The numbers in this list are *increasing*: 2, 3, 5, 9, 17.

Next, figure out the rate of increase:

```
2,   3,   5,   9,   17
 \_/  \_/  \_/  \_/
 +1   +2   +4   +8
```

Notice that, in this question, the rate of increase is not constant. The question needs to be solved by looking for a pattern in the rate of increase.

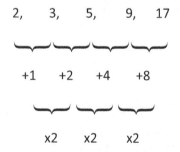

1, 2, 4, and 8 are all *multiples of 2*: $1 \times 2 = 2, 2 \times 2 = 4, 4 \times 2 = 8$. What is needed to continue this pattern? 8×2.

Given that $8 \times 2 = 16$, 16 is the next number in the rate of increase.

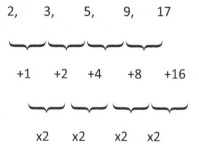

So, 16 must be added to the last number in the list to find the answer: $17 + 16 = 33$. The answer is B, 33.

Similar Words

In **similar words** questions, there will be a set of four words. Three of the words will be similar, and one will be different. The goal is to choose the one word that is *unlike* the other three.

The key to answering these questions correctly is to e*stablish the relationship between the three similar words.* The word that does not share that relationship with the others will be the answer. Here's an example:

> Three of the following words are similar, while one is different. Select the word that is different.
> a. Pants
> b. Closet
> c. Dresses
> d. Skirts

First, consider what the theme of the words is. The theme of this list seems to be *clothing.* Next, start with Choice *A* and consider how this word relates to Choice *B*. Pants can *be kept* in a closet.

In Choices *C* and *D*, dresses and skirts, like pants, can also be kept in a closet. So, three out of four of the words are articles of clothing that can be kept in a closet, rendering *closet* the word that is unlike the others. The answer is *B*, Closet.

Here's another example:

> Three of the following words are similar, while one is different. Select the word that is different.
> a. Book
> b. Magazine
> c. Newspaper
> d. Reading

In this question, the theme is *reading*, which is also one of the answer choices. Choices *A*, *B*, and *C* are things that can be read. Though Choice *D*, reading, does relate to the other answer choices, it does not relate in the same way. Reading is a verb, not an object that can be read, so the word that does not belong is *D*, Reading.

Practice Quiz

1. Theft can be defined as the act of taking something from another person without permission. Which of the following police situations would apply to this definition?
    a. A wife reports that her husband threw a plate and hit her.
    b. A dog is reported missing.
    c. A man reports that the window of his car was broken and his jacket is missing from the car.
    d. A cat is stuck in a tree.

2. A man exposes his body without any clothing in a public restaurant during peak business hours. Which of the following definitions applies to the incident?
    a. Public indecency
    b. Domestic abuse
    c. Theft
    d. Drug possession

3. Officer Skylor is reading reports about crimes that occur in his patrol area.

    All drug deals reported occur between 19th Avenue and 45th Avenue, all house break-ins occur in the neighborhoods between Roosevelt and Van Buren, and all vehicle break-ins occur by the strip mall along Lakeshore School Road.

    Most drug deals happen on Fridays, most house break-ins occur on Mondays, and most vehicle break-ins occur on Wednesdays.

    Most drug deals happen between 8:00 p.m. and midnight, most house break-ins occur between 10:00 a.m. and 2:00 p.m., and most vehicle break-ins occur between 5:00 p.m. and 9:00 p.m.

Officer Skylor will have the best chance of decreasing vehicle break-ins if he patrols which of the following?
    a. The strip mall along Lakeshore School Road on Wednesdays from 4:00 p.m. to 10:00 p.m.
    b. The strip mall along Lakeshore School Road on Fridays from 7:00 p.m. to 1:00 a.m.
    c. The neighborhoods between Roosevelt and Van Buren on Monday from 9:00 a.m. to 3:00 p.m.
    d. Between 19th Avenue and 45th Avenue from 4:00 p.m. to 10:00 p.m.

4. Officer Tiffany is reading the crime reports in her patrol area.

    All drug deals reported occur between 19th Avenue and 45th Avenue, all house break-ins occur in the neighborhoods between Roosevelt and Van Buren, and all vehicle break-ins occur by the strip mall along Lakeshore School Road.

    Most drug deals happen on Fridays, most house break-ins occur on Mondays, and most vehicle break-ins occur on Wednesdays.

    Most drug deals happen between 8:00 p.m. and midnight, most house break-ins occur between 10:00 a.m. and 2:00 p.m., and most vehicle break-ins occur between 5:00 p.m. and 9:00 p.m.

Officer Tiffany will have the best chance of decreasing house break-ins if she patrols which of the following?
   a. The neighborhoods between Roosevelt and Van Buren on Monday from 4:00 p.m. to 10:00 p.m.
   b. The strip mall along Lakeshore School Road on Fridays from 7:00 p.m. to 1:00 a.m.
   c. The neighborhoods between Roosevelt and Van Buren on Monday from 9:00 a.m. to 3:00 p.m.
   d. Between 19th Avenue and 45th Avenue from 9:00 a.m. to 3:00 p.m.

5. Officer Ryan is looking over his patrol area's crime reports.

   Most stolen goods are sold between 10:00 p.m. and 2:00 a.m., most drug deals occur between 10:00 p.m. and 2:00 a.m., and most muggings occur between 9:00 p.m. and midnight.

   Most illegal goods are sold on Fridays, most drug deals occur on Saturdays, and most muggings occur on Saturdays.

   Illegal goods are reported to be sold between Cherry Avenue and Missouri Avenue, drug deals occur in the Conant Gardens neighborhood, and muggings occur by the dollar store off Interstate 40.

Officer Ryan will have the best chance of decreasing muggings if he patrols which of the following?
   a. The Conant Gardens neighborhood on Saturdays from 9:00 p.m. to 3:00 a.m.
   b. The dollar store off Interstate 40 on Saturdays from 8:00 p.m. to 1:00 a.m.
   c. Between Cherry Avenue and Missouri Avenue on Saturdays from 8:00 p.m. to 1:00 a.m.
   d. Between Cherry Avenue and Missouri Avenue from 9:00 p.m. to 3:00 a.m.

See answers on next page.

Answer Explanations

1. C: The man's jacket missing is the only incident where a person's personal property was taken. Choices *A, B,* and *D* do not match this definition of theft.

2. A: A man exposing himself in public is the only situation that matches the definition of public indecency. Choices *B, C,* and *D* have definitions that relate to different crimes.

3. A: The question specifically asks for when vehicle break-ins occur; therefore, to determine the correct choice, the data that relates specifically to vehicle break-ins should be examined. From the given information, most vehicle break-ins happen at the strip mall along Lakeshore School Road on Wednesdays from 5:00 p.m. to 9:00 p.m., so the best time to prevent these break-ins would be to arrive at the location an hour early and stay an hour later to catch all potential break-ins.

4. C: This question is regarding only house break-ins, which, according to the data given, occur between Roosevelt and Van Buren on Mondays from 10:00 a.m. to 2:00 p.m. The remaining choices, although the time or day may be correct, do not list the correct area according to the report.

5. B: This question is regarding only muggings, which, according to the data given, occur by the dollar store off Interstate 40 on Saturdays between 9:00 p.m. and midnight. The remaining choices, although the time or day may be correct, do not list the correct area according to the report.

Personal Characteristics/Behavioral Attributes

For the behavioral attributes questions on the CJBAT, there are no correct or incorrect answers. You will be given a rating scale from 1 to 5:

- Strongly agree: 1
- Agree: 2
- Not sure: 3
- Disagree: 4
- Strongly disagree: 5

With this rating scale, you will answer from 1 to 5 your response to each statement. The questions may assess your behavior in certain situations, your anxiety levels, or how you compare yourself to others. Respond to each statement as honestly as you can. The following sections are designed to help you understand why behavior and police response are important in law enforcement.

Finding the Most Appropriate Response

A police scenario can be any number of instances that are related to a case. An officer needs to be ready to make the most appropriate responses based on a combination of their training and reasoning abilities. An officer's actions should not only help to solve cases but should be made to first and foremost ensure the safety of those involved. Each police scenario will be different, so it may be difficult sometimes to decide what the correct course of action might be. Decisions also need to be made quickly in the event a scenario necessitates an immediate response. An officer will also be required to analyze and interpret data involved from multiple sources to fully understand other situations to make informed conclusions.

The first step to finding appropriate responses for a police scenario requires the collection and analyzation of data so the officer can be properly informed on the situation. The most useful data will be the honest facts, and therefore details will need to be researched to confirm the veracity of the data. If a more immediate action is needed, the officer will have to pay close attention to all the surrounding details and take note of anyone who is in immediate danger. Actions must be backed up based on the facts of the case later. After examining the details, an officer should think of several different actions that could be taken. These options should be contrasted with each other to determine which action would best fit the situation. The final decision should be the one that most conforms to the law and is the safest course of action to prevent danger in the field.

Human Psychology and Behavior

There are many different theoretical perspectives to explain human behavior. The following are some of the most prevalent approaches to understanding human behavior.

The **systems approach** seeks to evaluate and explain human behavior as the individual interacts with the different social systems that they are a part of, including the family, community, and work environment. The systems approach emphasizes the importance of a person's perceived role in society or family, such as father, wife, or student. The Stanford Prison Experiment of 1971 confirmed the importance of social roles, when students—who were given the roles of guards and prisoners in a simulated prison experience—began to dramatically and even dangerously adopt those roles.

Another important theory to explain human behavior is the **conflict theory**, which focuses on division of power, oppression, and conflict between social groups and within social systems, and what happens when groups or people have competing interests. Recently in social work, with an increased emphasis on social justice, the conflict theory has gained more influence as it looks at dominant and privileged groups as contrasted with oppressed and underprivileged populations.

The **rational choice** or **social exchange perspective** explains human behavior in the context of the social give and take of resources. Each person is making rational choices in their interactions with others, primarily motivated by selfish reasons and with the desire to minimize costs to themselves, while maximizing the benefits received.

The **social constructionist perspective** has to do with how people derive meaning from their world and how they analyze and classify society around them. Socially and culturally, shared understandings are developed about people and their places in the world, which leads to an ever-changing social construct.

The **psychodynamic theory**, built on Freud's work, emphasizes the unconscious and internal drives and motives that rule human behavior. Some other important components of the psychodynamic perspective are the significance of childhood experiences and the use of defense mechanisms as a means of protection from unacceptable feelings and impulses.

As previously discussed, the **developmental perspective** looks at how humans grow and change throughout their lifespan and the impact that this has on human behavior. At each stage of life, there are different emotional, physical, and psychological changes that occur, and there are different developmental tasks that must be overcome.

Another way of explaining human behavior is the **social learning perspective**, built on the idea that people learn how to behave as they interact with their environment. This learning may take place through classical conditioning, which is the development of automatic responses to stimuli in the environment, or operant conditioning, in which the behaviors that are rewarded increase, and the behaviors that are punished decrease. The third form of learning is observational learning, which explains how people learn the behaviors that are modeled for them.

Finally, **the humanistic approach** emphasizes the uniqueness, individuality, free will, and value of each human being. Human behavior is viewed as an attempt to reach toward self-actualization and to find a sense of purpose and fulfillment. Abraham Maslow, a renowned humanist psychologist, developed his hierarchy of needs to explain the human progression from having basic needs met to becoming self-transcendent.

Strengths-Based and Resilience Theories

Rather than focusing on problems and pathology, the strengths perspective (or **strengths-based approach**) in social work encourages social workers to focus on a client's strengths or assets and to build upon the client's inherent resiliency and positive characteristics. Outcome studies regarding use of the strengths perspective are limited. However, it is posited that a strength-based approach could help to remove some of the stigma attached to groups or to conditions (e.g., mental illness, poverty).

Defense Mechanisms and Human Behavior

Sigmund Freud's **psychoanalytic theory** focused on the conflicts, drives, and unacceptable desires in the unconscious mind and how they affect a person. One method of dealing with unconscious conflicts is through **defense mechanisms**, which are the mind's way of protecting a person from unacceptable thoughts. Here are some of the most common defense mechanisms:

- **Repression** is when a person suppresses thoughts or memories that are too difficult to handle. They are pushed out of the conscious mind, and a person may experience memory loss or have psychogenic amnesia related to those memories.

- **Displacement** takes place when someone displaces the feelings that they have toward one person, such as anger, and puts it on another person who may be less threatening. For example, someone may express anger toward a spouse, but the person that they are truly angry at is their boss.

- **Sublimation** is when the socially unacceptable thought is transformed into healthy, acceptable behavior in another direction. Pain may become poetry, for example.

- **Rationalization** is when unacceptable feelings or thoughts are rationally and logically explained and defended.

- **Reaction formation** occurs when the negative feeling is covered up by a false or exaggerated version of its opposite. In such a case, a person may display strong feelings of affection toward someone, though internally and unconsciously hate that person.

- **Denial** is refusing to accept painful facts or situations and instead acting as if they are not true or have not happened.

- **Projection** is putting one's own feelings onto someone else and acting as if they are the one who feels that way instead of oneself.

Group Theories

The following is a list of groups in social work that individuals use for greater social functioning and fellowship in order to learn better coping skills.

The **Mutual Aid Model** is derived from theoretical work by social work pioneer, William Schwartz. This model is also referred to as self-help or support groups. Clients within the group need and help each other as they tackle problems that are common across group members. This model is commonly used with groups focused on substance abuse.

Cognitive-behavioral group work utilizes cognitive-behavioral therapy (CBT) interventions, initially used in individual work and applies those interventions to a group setting. Although mutual aid is not emphasized or a core component, group discussion is valued, and group members do interact with each other. The focus is on learning skills and changing behavior in order for individuals to function more effectively.

Systems-Centered therapy groups are based on the work of Yvonne Agazarian (*Theory of Living Human Systems*). Human systems have energy and use that energy for survival, development, and mastery of the environment. Group members use functional subgrouping to work together, explore similarities and differences, learn perspective taking, and resolve conflicts.

Interpersonal Learning Groups were made well known by Irvin Yalom, a pioneer in group theory and practice. This approach uses group interaction as the mechanism for achieving awareness, insight, and change. The leader of the group must facilitate interpersonal learning.

Systems and Ecological Perspectives

Systems Theory in social work refers to the view that human behavior is explained by the influences of the various systems to which individuals belong. When evaluating and conceptualizing an individual's behavior, that behavior must be considered in the context of the individual's family, society, and other systems.

- All systems are seen as possessing interrelated parts and exerting influence on each other.
- There are many iterations of the premise of the basic systems theory.
- In practice, systems theory allows a social worker to better understand the dynamics of a client's systems while also creating an appropriate intervention approach.
- The originator of systems theory in social work was Ludwig von Bertalanffy, a biologist who was influenced by sociologists Max Weber and Emile Durkheim.

Talcott Parsons expanded on earlier work with his framework of **structural functionalism**, which proposes that a system is defined by its function in its social environment.

Four states of social systems:

- Adaptation to the social environment
- Goal attainment
- Integration with other systems
- Latency or homeostasis (social patterns and norms are maintained)

Designations of social systems in social work:

- Microsystems: small systems (e.g., an individual or a couple)
- Mezzosystems: medium-sized systems (e.g., extended families, groups to which the individual belongs)
- Macrosystems: large systems (e.g., organizations, communities)

The **ecological systems perspective** is concerned with the transactions between systems:

- People and families must be considered within cultural and societal contexts, which also necessitates examining the events that have occurred in an individual's life.
- Changes made by the individual that cause the entire system to shift must also be considered.

Common interventions based on systems theory:

- Strengthening a part of the system in order to improve the whole system
- Creating a genogram: a family tree constructed with a client in order to improve understanding of the familial relationships and to identify recurring patterns

- Connecting clients to organizations or individuals who can help them to function better within and between their systems

- Developing an ecomap: an illustration of client's systems, such as family and community and how it changes over time

Person-in-Environment

Carel Germain described person-in-environment interaction based upon earlier work in systems theory. This perspective takes into consideration an individual's environmental and systemic influences. It is specific to social work, which differentiates it from other like professions.

- Life stress: the normal tension that occurs as the result of both external demands and internal experiences. What is experienced as stressful varies across people and their perceptions. For example, two people placed in the same environment may have completely different experiences due to the ways in which they experience and perceive the situation.

- Adaptation: when the environment and the individual change in response to the interaction with each other

- Coping: individual use of one's own strengths and problem-solving abilities to navigate life stress and develop self-esteem and hope

- Power: can be a source of stress to individuals as well as the larger system when misused by certain groups

- Human relatedness: the ability of individuals to cultivate relationships

- Three related concepts are *self-direction*, *competence*, and *self-esteem*. These attributes are interdependent and occur cross-culturally.

Impact of Social Institutions on Society

Social institutions exist to meet the needs of individuals, promote pro-social behavior, define social norms, and create order.

There are five major social institutions:

Family
- Regulates sexual behavior (monogamy)
- Creates and provides for new society members
- Socializes new society members

Religion
- Provides explanations for the unexplainable
- Supports societal norms and values
- Provides a means of coping with life situations

Government
- Institutionalizes norms (by creating laws)
- Enforces laws

Personal Characteristics/Behavioral Attributes

- Protects members of society
- Provides a means of resolving conflict

Education
- Prepares society members to contribute to the society in specified roles
- Teaches skills necessary to function within the society

Economics
- Produces and distributes goods needed by society members
- Provides services necessary to the society

Social Change and Community Development Theories

Community development theory focuses on oppressed people who are in the process of overcoming social problems that were imposed upon them by external forces. In the process of community development, members of a community learn how to improve that community and gain control of their local environment. **Community-level change** brings people together and demonstrates the power of solidarity. This theory also acknowledges the reality that many problems are at the social, rather than individual, level. An implication of the theory is that therapy addresses only the symptoms of a problem and not the underlying causes.

Influence of Social Context on Behavior

There are many ways in which a social context can influence individual behavior, either positively or negatively. Social psychology looks at the person-environment interaction and explores the many ways the social setting influences a person's attitudes and actions.

Attitudes toward, and influenced by, those around play a major role in a person's behaviors. **Attribution theory** has to do with how one views the behavior of others, whether attributing their behaviors to disposition or situation. If one wrongly attributes someone's negative action to their disposition—the **fundamental attribution error**—then one may think more negatively about others than is deserved.

The concept of **conformity**—the tendency for a person to conform personal behaviors to the behaviors of those around them—helps explain everything from style trends to mass genocide. Solomon Asch performed a study that showed that people tend to conform to the people around them, even if it means giving an answer they know is false. The phenomenon of conformity stems from the idea that people act in a way to get approval from others and to avoid disapproval, called **normative social influence**. Another impact of the social sphere that people live in is **deindividuation**, in which a person loses a sense of personal responsibility or individualism. This may happen in crowds at a concert or sports event, or a riot, leading people to behave in ways they would not normally behave if they did not feel anonymous and emotionally charged by the social setting.

People tend to automatically form groups, often developing the in-group and out-group concepts. The **in-group** consists of those who are part of the group, who share its identity and unifying characteristics. The **out-group** consists of those outside the group, particularly those who may be in opposition or share opposite beliefs to those in the in-group. This in-group and out-group concept may lead to patriotism or working together towards a common goal, but it may also lead to prejudice and discrimination. Groups also tend to engage in **group think**, where no one is willing to share an opinion contrary to the group, or **group polarization**, in which people in the group become stronger and stronger in their opinions as they spend time with others who have similar beliefs.

Some other key concepts related to the effects of social context on behavior are social loafing and social facilitation. **Social loafing** happens in a context of shared responsibility for a task. In this case, there is a tendency for some people to abdicate responsibility, assuming that others will fulfill the obligations of the work. **Social facilitation**, on the other hand, is when having an audience inspires people to perform tasks they do well even better. Alternatively, it can also cause them to do worse in tasks they find more difficult or challenging.

Leadership

Quality leadership skills are essential to any organization, and thus, leadership training is typically provided to mid and upper management. Signs of effective leadership skills are strategic thinking, solving problems as they come, and managing time in the most financially responsible manner. While these skills are essential, there are also more human characteristics that must be mentioned. A successful leader must have the ability to: build confidence within his or her team or organization, obtain the trust of others, inspire others, and engender a sense of pride and purpose within his or her company.

Management and Leadership Development

Management and leadership development is a critical component for organizations to invest in. For this practice to be effective, managers must exercise their capacities to establish objectives and means of attainment. Concurrently, management and leadership development is designed to equip the workforce with the requisite tools and skills to compete in a functional organization. The primary purpose of management and leadership development is to provide a holistic approach for individuals, managers, and leadership. Individuals are able to increase their skills and knowledge working within an organizational apparatus. Managers find more efficient ways to execute predetermined objectives. Leaders improve their ability in a decision-making process that incorporates creative input from the organization's members and accomplishes mutually shared goals.

Equal Employment Practices

Equal employment practices (EEP) are ways employers and human resource administrators can ensure best practices are put to use when hiring, training, and retaining employees. Equal employment opportunity was first put into place to prevent discrimination against race or color. Furthering equal employment opportunity was the Executive Order 11246 signed by Lyndon B. Johnson in order to prohibit discrimination against race, sex, creed, religion, color, or national origin. More protected classes have been added to the order, including age and Americans with disabilities, among others.

The U.S. government has an Equal Opportunity Commission website with a list on how to prevent discrimination. On the site, it mentions that human resource managers should train employees on EEO laws, encourage an inclusive culture, and foster open communication in order to prevent and manage disputes. They also promote hiring workers from a diverse pool of applicants and that the criteria in selecting an employee should not disproportionately exclude a certain race, unless "the criteria are valid predictors of successful job performance and meet the employer's business needs." All employees should have equal access to workplace networks, and compensation practices should be monitored by the employers to ensure fair ratings.

Practice Quiz

Use the following scale to respond to each statement as you see fit. Use the scale below.

- Strongly agree: 1
- Agree: 2
- Not sure: 3
- Disagree: 4
- Strongly disagree: 5

1. I feel like a failure when I do not meet my goals.

2. When I'm in groups working on a project, I usually take the lead.

3. Communicating with others is one of my strongest attributes.

4. It is normal for people to become angry in tense situations.

5. I am sometimes nervous in situations I have never been in before.

See answers on next page.

Answer Explanations

Answers will vary from 1 to 5.

Practice Test #1

Memorization

Directions for the next five questions:

Examine the image below for two minutes then remove it from view. Answer the questions that follow the image without referring back to the image. Do not read the questions during the image review period.

1. How many people are in the room on the middle right?
   a. 1
   b. 2
   c. 3
   d. 4

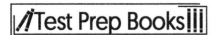

2. How many cameras are there?
   a. 4
   b. 3
   c. 2
   d. 1

3. Which of the following items is in the room at the top?
   a. Stool
   b. Clock
   c. Camera
   d. Flag

4. What time is it on the clock?
   a. 11:15
   b. 1:55
   c. 10:30
   d. 2:35

5. How many officers are checking in at the bottom check-in station?
   a. 2
   b. 1
   c. 4
   d. 3

Practice Test #1

Directions for the next five questions:

Examine the image below for two minutes then remove it from view. Answer the questions that follow the image without referring back to the image. Do not read the questions during the image review period.

6. How many lanes of traffic are there?
   a. 3
   b. 6
   c. 4
   d. 2

7. How many miles are there until the exit 8?
   a. 1
   b. 3
   c. 4
   d. 6

8. What is hanging from the rearview mirror of the compact car?
    a. A basketball
    b. An air freshener
    c. A disco ball
    d. A soccer ball

9. Approximately how many cars are in the image?
    a. 10-15
    b. 15-20
    c. 20-30
    d. 30-40

10. How many airbags deployed in the accident?
    a. 1
    b. 2
    c. 3
    d. 4

Practice Test #1

Directions for the next five questions:

Examine the image below for two minutes then remove it from view. Answer the questions that follow the image without referring back to the image. Do not read the questions during the image review period.

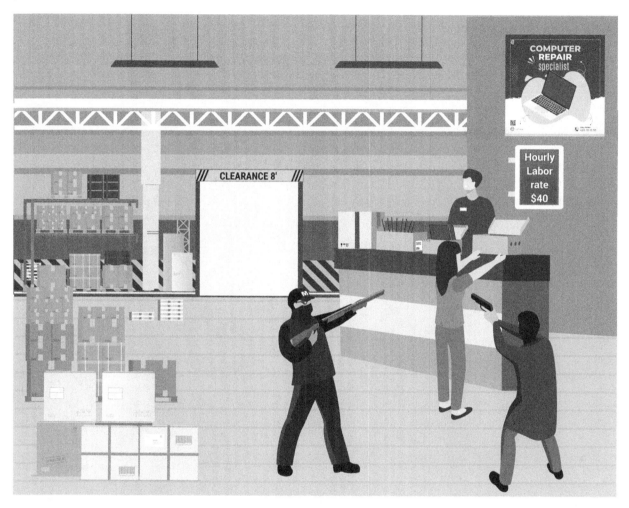

11. What is the hourly labor rate?
    a. 60/hr
    b. 40/hr
    c. 30/hr
    d. 50/hr

12. What letter is on one of the gunmen's baseball hat?
    a. V
    b. W
    c. S
    d. M

13. How many boxes are on the counter?
    a. 4
    b. 3
    c. 6
    d. 5

14. How many boxes are open?
    a. 4
    b. 1
    c. 2
    d. 3

15. How tall is the doorway?
    a. 6 feet
    b. 9 feet
    c. 8 feet
    d. 7 feet

Practice Test #1

Directions for the next five questions:

Examine the image below for two minutes then remove it from view. Answer the questions that follow the image without referring back to the image. Do not read the questions during the image review period.

16. According to the sign in the door, how many hours is the store open on Sunday?
    a. 12
    b. 8
    c. 11
    d. 10

17. What item is visible in the shopping bags?
    a. Eggs
    b. Toilet paper
    c. Steak
    d. Milk

18. What is written on the man's shirt?
    a. Sun
    b. Smile
    c. Surf
    d. Shore

19. What is the bicycle missing?
    a. Seat
    b. Tire
    c. Chain
    d. Lock

20. What item is the woman wearing?
    a. Pants
    b. Skirt
    c. Shorts
    d. A long coat

Use the map below to answer questions 21 and 22:

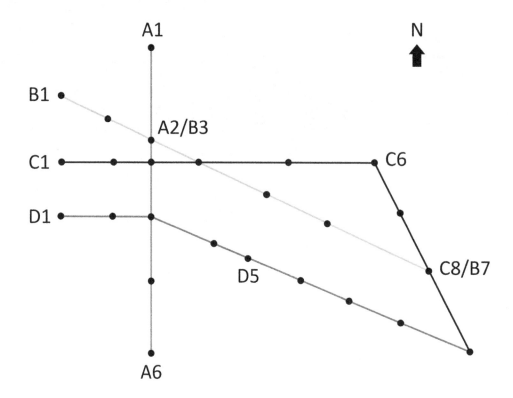

21. The map above shows the routes of subway lines in the city. Each color represents a different subway route, and each route is also labeled with a letter. Each stop in the route is identified by a black dot and a number that starts at either the western-most or northern-most stop, increasing by one at each following stop.

Practice Test #1

If Mr. Smith wants to commute from stop A2 to C9, which route would be the quickest (go through the least number of stops)?
   a. A2 to C4 to B7 to C9
   b. A2 to C4 to C6 to C9
   c. A2 to C3 to C6 to C9
   d. A2 to D3 to C9

22. The map above shows the routes of subway lines in the city. Each color represents a different subway route, and each route is also labeled with a letter. Each stop in the route is identified by a black dot and a number that starts at either the western-most or northern-most stop, increasing by one at each following stop.

Mr. Smith needs to get from stop A6 to B7, but the C line is closed off for the day. Which route would be the LEAST efficient to take (go through the greatest number of stops) but still get Mr. Smith to his destination?
   a. A6 to D3 to D8 to B7
   b. A6 to A2 to B7
   c. A6 to C3 to C6 to B7
   d. A6 to C3 to B4 to B5 to B7

Use the map below to answer questions 23 and 24:

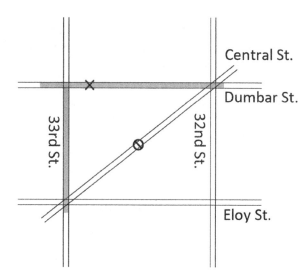

23. The map above shows the amount of traffic in a given area. The double lines indicate roads and the ones shaded grey indicate roads with heavier traffic. A crash is indicated by the symbol ✕. Closed roads are indicated with a ⊘.

According to the traffic depiction, if you were at the corner of Eloy St. and 32nd St., which route would be the fastest way to the crash site?
   a. 32nd Street to Dumbar Street
   b. 35th Street to Dumbar Street
   c. Eloy Street to 33rd Street
   d. Eloy Street to 31st Street to Dumbar Street

24. The map above shows the amount of traffic in a given area. The double lines indicate roads and the ones shaded grey indicate roads with heavier traffic. A crash is indicated by the symbol ✗. Closed roads are indicated with a 🚫.

If the black dot on the graph above represents the officer's current location, which route would have the least amount of traffic to take to the grey dot?
   a. Dumbar Street to 33rd Street to destination
   b. 32nd Street to Eloy Street to destination
   c. Central Street to destination
   d. Dumbar Street to 31st Street to Eloy Street to destination

25. Which of the following facial features would be the MOST recognizable when asked to match a face with a sketch?
   a. Medium-length hair
   b. A smiling face
   c. A cigarette in the mouth
   d. A birthmark below the eye

Written Comprehension

The next two questions are based on the following passage:

> The majority of records that are taken as part of court proceedings are considered part of the public domain, and are therefore available to anyone who requests access. These documents can be used to conduct background checks, revealing information such as age, marital status, military status, and whether a person has ever been convicted of a crime. While many records are made public, some are sealed by a judge for extraordinary circumstances, such as to protect the privacy of a minor. Each state has its own rules governing which records can be accessed and counties determine how. In some cases, the records can be obtained through a quick search of a state or county database, but others will require a request of the appropriate department. For example, in the state of California, most court records can be accessed through county court databases, but Supreme and Appellate Court records are only available from the Appellate Court.

1. Based on the preceding passage, which of the following statements is most accurate?
   a. All court records can be accessed via online databases.
   b. Court records are always part of the public domain, so they can be accessed by anyone.
   c. Military status is private, so it cannot be revealed in court documents.
   d. For various reasons, some documents are sealed, so they are not accessible to the public.

2. Based on the preceding passage, which of the following statements is most accurate?
   a. Each state determines how and when court records can be accessed by the public.
   b. A judge should seal all court records for minors.
   c. A judge can seal a court record for any reason.
   d. California allows all court records to be accessed by county record databases.

The next two questions are based on the following passage:

Conducting a traffic stop can be one of the most dangerous parts of being a police officer. In light of the many traffic stop incidents that have occurred all over the country, many states are looking at how to address the problem. Recently, the state of Illinois passed a new law that adds traffic stop training to their driver's education courses. These courses are aimed to make new drivers prepared for all the possibilities of the road, and a potential traffic stop by a police officer is one of those possibilities. Proponents of traffic stop training say that this could help new drivers, especially young teens, not to panic in the event they get pulled over. If they know what to expect and how to handle a traffic stop, it is hoped that they could protect themselves from doing anything that could be perceived as a threat, such as reaching under the seat or arguing with the officer. As this new driver's education component gains popularity, it could be seen in more states across the US, and hopefully it will reduce the amount of traffic stop incidents.

3. Based on the preceding passage, which of the following statements is most accurate?
    a. A new law in Illinois makes it required for all drivers to take driver's education courses.
    b. Lawmakers believe that traffic stop training will help police officers stop more underage drivers.
    c. Arguing with an officer is illegal during a traffic stop.
    d. The new law in Illinois adds traffic stop training to driver's education courses.

4. Based on the preceding passage, which of the following statements is most accurate?
    a. Traffic stops are not dangerous.
    b. Police officers can teach new drivers how to act when they are pulled over.
    c. Traffic stop training aims to protect young drivers from panicking when they are pulled over.
    d. Young drivers should not worry about being pulled over if they are driving safely.

The next two questions are based on the following passage:

Federal law does not restrict the open carry of a weapon in public. Each state determines its own open carry laws. While there are some restrictions to these laws—such as requiring permits or prohibiting weapons in certain locations like schools or on public transportation—most states allow the open carry of a handgun. Currently, 31 states allow private citizens to open carry a firearm without a license. Only three states, California, Florida, and Illinois, and the District of Columbia, prohibit open carry of a firearm. Concealed carry refers to carrying a firearm under clothing or in a way that is not visible to the casual observer. Every state and the District of Columbia allow the concealed carry of a firearm in some form. Forty-two states do require a permit for concealed carry. Of these 42 states, some have a "may issue" law that allows for wider denial of the permit. Other states have a "shall issue" law, which generally accepts most permits without discretion.

5. Based on the preceding passage, which of the following statements is most accurate?
    a. Open carry laws are strict in all 50 states.
    b. Only California, Florida, and Illinois allow for open carry of a firearm without a permit.
    c. Nineteen states require a permit for open carry of a firearm.
    d. Most states allow for open carry of a firearm with limited restrictions.

6. Based on the preceding passage, which of the following statements is most accurate?
   a. Eight states require a permit for concealed carry of a firearm in public.
   b. States that have a "may issue" law have very little restrictions on who can get a concealed carry permit.
   c. All states allow for the concealed carry of a firearm in public.
   d. States that have a "shall issue" law have strict restrictions on who can carry a weapon.

The next two questions are based on the following passage:

Since the 1966 Supreme *Court case*, Miranda v. Arizona, police officers have been required to read the Miranda rights, or Miranda warning, to any person taken into police custody. The Miranda rights include the following:

- You have the right to remain silent.
- Anything you say can and will be used against you in a court of law.
- You have the right to an attorney.
- If you cannot afford an attorney, one will be appointed for you.

To fully comply with Miranda rights, the person in custody must also waive their rights, typically in writing. If they do not waive their rights, any information they provide is not admissible in court. Police officers are required to read these rights so that the person in custody is aware of them, but also to protect the information that is given in any questioning they might conduct. When a person in custody is not Mirandized, anything they say, such as a confession or the location of evidence, cannot be used in court.

7. Based on the preceding passage, which of the following statements is most accurate?
   a. The Miranda rights require the person in custody to remain silent.
   b. The Miranda rights are the result of a Supreme Court case.
   c. Police officers are not always required to read the Miranda rights to a person in custody.
   d. The Miranda rights tell the person in custody that they don't need a lawyer.

8. Based on the preceding passage, which of the following statements is most accurate?
   a. Miranda rights only protect the person in custody.
   b. Police officers who do not read Miranda rights to a person in custody can be sued.
   c. A person must waive their Miranda rights in order for the information they provide to be admissible in court.
   d. Any information gained from a person in custody who has not waived their Miranda rights can be used in court.

The next two questions are based on the following passage:

Many police departments have begun using social media outlets such as Twitter, Facebook, and Instagram to their benefit. Police departments have found that the use of social media can be very helpful in identifying suspects, alerting the community to a possible threat, locating a missing person, and even gaining support for their organization. Social media is a two-way street, so police departments are also able to get valuable information and feedback from the communities they serve. Departments who use social media report that when their community feels like they have a forum to voice their opinion, it creates a sense of trust in the police. Departments that do opt to use social media should abide by some simple rules, such as limiting the amount of information released, especially on ongoing cases, using appropriate language, and having a single point of contact to manage the sites for continuity. Social media can be a great asset to any police department if used appropriately.

9. Based on the preceding passage, which of the following statements is most accurate?
    a. Police departments should make a Facebook page but avoid Twitter and Instagram.
    b. Social media has been helpful to police departments in identifying suspects and locating missing persons.
    c. Community trust is not built through the use of social media outlets.
    d. Social media can be helpful to police departments, but it is not used very often.

10. Based on the preceding passage, which of the following statements is most accurate?
    a. Police departments should try to use a single person to manage social media pages.
    b. Police departments should make full use of social media by revealing the details of ongoing cases.
    c. Social media is not beneficial in ongoing cases.
    d. Police departments that want to use social media should hire a consultant to set up their sites.

The next two questions are based on the following passage:

When it comes to violent crime, one of the most important aspects of identifying and convicting a suspect is the collection of evidence. There are several steps in the process of collecting physical evidence including being able to identify what on or near a crime scene should and can be considered evidence. Crime scene investigators are trained in identifying latent prints; footwear and tire tracks; biological, drug, firearm, trace and digital evidence; and tool and tool mark evidence. Once evidence is identified, it must be collected, maintained, and stored in a way that ensures the integrity of the evidence. More specifically, investigators must wear gloves and change them as necessary to ensure there is no contamination, store items separately and in appropriate containers also avoiding cross-contamination, seal and initial the items with a date and time stamp, and then carefully monitor the chain of custody. Failure to adhere to the very stringent rules of evidence collection and storage can jeopardize the use of that evidence should the case come to trial.

11. Based on the preceding passage, which statement is most accurate?
    a. How evidence is stored is not as important as how it's collected.
    b. Avoiding cross-contamination is one of the most important elements of evidence collection.
    c. Crime scene investigators are ultimately responsible for a prosecutor's success in convicting a suspect.
    d. Collecting everything from a crime scene is a strategy used by crime scene investigators.

12. Handling evidence at a crime scene is an important process. It includes which step listed here:
    a. Identifying a suspect
    b. Avoiding cross-contamination
    c. Monitoring the chain of custody
    d. Wearing gloves

The next two questions are based on the following passage:

Eyewitnesses are essential to crime scene investigations. Not only can they help identify suspects, but their information may be useful in charging and convicting an individual as well. For that reason, how a law enforcement officer questions this individual is of the utmost importance. Because witnesses to crimes are human and how the human brain stores information is sometimes unreliable, procedures have been developed to ensure officers are able to effectively collect and preserve eyewitness evidence. One of the first goals is that, when making first contact with the witness, the dispatcher should gather information from the witness in a way that is not suggestive or leading. Questions, throughout the entire evidence gathering process, should be open ended, allowing the witness to provide information as it comes to them. Follow-up questions may be more specific and ask for details based on initial answers. Therefore, they may be close ended. For example, if the witness says they saw a car, it is appropriate to ask what color or type of car they saw. In contrast, a leading or suggestive question might offer a color to the witness rather than waiting for them to answer, such as "Was it the car blue?" Additionally, to prevent contamination of eye witness evidence, officers responding to a scene should separate witness and make it clear that it's inappropriate for them to discuss what they saw.

13. Based on the above passage, why is it important to ask open ended questions?
    a. Open-ended questions allow you to ask follow-up questions.
    b. Open-ended questions are only effective if followed by a close ended question.
    c. Open-ended questions allow the witness to provide information without leading them.
    d. Open-ended questions allow you to lead the witness to useful information.

14. Based on the above passage, what should a responding officer do with witnesses?
    a. Suggest they discuss what they saw to create a full picture.
    b. Immediately gather information using open ended questions.
    c. Get their names and information and allow them to leave.
    d. Separate them to avoid contamination of the evidence.

The next three questions are based on the following passage:

Writing a police report may seem simple, but there is a big difference between writing a police report and writing a good police report. Above all, good reports are organized and clear. To write the best report possible, those two elements are paramount. Unfortunately, organization is often a challenge and when organization is non-linear, clarity can be lost as well. More specifically, when combining multiple stories from multiple people relaying what happened to them, what they witnessed, and even what the writer witnessed upon arrival, each story has a different starting point. That raises a fundamental question regarding organization. In what order does one tell the "story?" Opening with a statement that includes the reporter's name, date, time the call was received, the location, and the crime reported is a good way to start. It sets the stage and allows the writer to create a clear organizational structure. Next, the writer will want to introduce all the pertinent people and locations. From there, the writer can then describe the actions that took place, in the order that they happened. Should an individual arrive midway into the action or sequence of events, their arrival is simply part of the order of events. At the end of the report, the writer will have an opportunity to include any other important information including evidence such as photos or property and statements from the victim, witnesses, and, perhaps, the suspect. Any other relevant facts can be added in at that time as well. In this way, writers can ensure they provide organized and clear reports.

15. What is one of the most important elements of writing good reports?
    a. Details
    b. Organization
    c. Concise
    d. Providing the victim's timeline

16. Based on the passage, what is one of the biggest challenges of organizing a report?
    a. Remembering to include all the evidence
    b. Remembering what each witness said
    c. Determining what facts are relevant
    d. Determining the timeline to use

17. The best time to include evidence in the report is:
    a. At the end with other relevant information
    b. When it might appear in the timeline
    c. At the start, it's best to lay out all the facts
    d. Evidence should be submitted as a separate report

The next three questions are based on the following passage:

There are plenty of aspects of a police career that can be scary. Any situation an officer enters into can change rapidly and, as a result, produce physiological responses that increase stress. However, one situation that causes stress even without the added uncertainty is testifying in a court case. Officers enter unknown situations daily, so why is it that testifying in a court case, when an officer knows what is expected, what will happen, and when it will be, still so anxiety-producing? In part, many officers might feel as if the entire case and a resulting conviction rest entirely on their shoulders. However, it's also possible that a fear of public speaking, which is quite common, creates issues as well. Further, it requires an officer to trust a prosecutor and to understand they have little control over questions from an opposing attorney or judge. When officers are typically used to being either in control or creating order, this can be stressful. However, there are steps one can take to mitigate the anxiety and fear. First, officers should review the facts of the case as well as applicable laws, policies, and procedures. Familiarity with this information will breed confidence. Few things reduce stress more than taking control of what you can control. Next, anxiety is sometimes created when we don't know what the other attorney knows. For example, if you are testifying, the attorney has likely gathered information on you, so it's best to let a prosecutor know if anything from your personnel file might turn up. Again, this comes down to controlling what you. Lastly, anticipate the questions you may be asked and practice answering yes, no, or I don't know. Attorneys may try to trip you up with multi-layered compound questions and you can ask for clarification. Control what you can and be prepared for what you can't so you can alleviate a lot of the stress associate with testifying.

18. Based on the above passage, which of these contributes to the stress of testifying?
    a. Lack of control
    b. Lack of information
    c. Lack of experience
    d. Lack of support

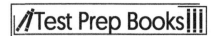

19. According to the passage, what is one step an officer can take to ease the anxiety associated with testifying?
    a. Research the attorneys and judge
    b. Sit in on trials
    c. Practice public speaking
    d. Review the facts of the case

20. According to the passage, what should officers tell prosecutors?
    a. The facts of the case
    b. What is in their personnel file
    c. What they learned about the attorney and judge
    d. Reveal that they have anxiety about testifying

Written Expression

Directions: In the following sentences, choose the correct spelling of the missing word. Mark the letter that identifies your choice on the answer sheet.

1. A non-violent breach of a law to bring about social change is called civil _____.
    a. disobidiance
    b. disobedense
    c. disobedience
    d. disobediance

2. After graduating from the police academy, you will be assigned to a _____.
    a. pricinct
    b. precint
    c. precinct
    d. presinct

3. Becoming a police officer is a great _____ to serve your community.
    a. oppurtinity
    b. opportunity
    c. opportinity
    d. oppurtunity

4. I _____ spilled coffee on my desk.
    a. acidentally
    b. assidentilly
    c. accidentilly
    d. accidentally

5. Your excellent work shows how _____ you are to the job.
    a. comited
    b. comitted
    c. commited
    d. committed

Directions: Read each sentence carefully and select the answer that is closest in meaning to the underlined word. Use prefix/suffix definitions and context clues to help eliminate incorrect answers.

6. The company treasurer was found guilty of <u>embezzling</u> $50,000 from the company's bank account to pay for the remodeling of his home.
    a. Bedazzling
    b. Stealing
    c. Decorating
    d. Borrowing

7. The judge <u>exonerated</u> Susan of all charges, so she left the courtroom a free woman.
    a. Cleared
    b. Executed
    c. Tried
    d. Convicted

8. When officers arrived on the scene of the deadly crash, they learned there had been one <u>fatality</u>.
    a. Birth
    b. Attraction
    c. Death
    d. Celebration

9. The unsuspecting art collector didn't realize the painting was a <u>forgery</u> until after it was appraised, so she became the 13th victim of the con artist.
    a. Antique
    b. Operation
    c. Sculpture
    d. Fake

10. The criminals wore gloves so they wouldn't leave behind any <u>latent</u> fingerprints.
    a. Hidden
    b. Painted
    c. Vinyl
    d. Visible

Reasoning

1. Which of the following is the next number in the series: 84, 80, 76, 72, 68...?
    a. 75
    b. 67
    c. 64
    d. 70

2. Which of the following is the next number in the series: 17, 18, 20, 23, 27...?
    a. 29
    b. 33
    c. 23
    d. 32

3. After school, Andrew, Matt and Geeta spend time watching television. Andrew watches more television than Geeta but less than Matt. Which of the following lists the friends in order from who watches the most television after school to who watches the least?
    a. Andrew, Matt, Geeta
    b. Not enough information
    c. Geeta, Andrew, Matt
    d. Matt, Andrew, Geeta

4. Three of the following words are similar, while one is different. Which one is different?
    a. Notebook
    b. Pencil
    c. Pen
    d. Crayon

5. Which of the following is the next number in the series: 41, 30, 42, 29, 43, 28...?
    a. 30
    b. 44
    c. 43
    d. 41

Use the table below to answer question 6:

Number of Cases by County in 2019			
County	Cases Filed	Cases Completed	Cases Completed Increase/Decrease From 2018
Maricopa	1512	1353	+276
Mohave	1289	1199	−105
Pima	1156	1044	−165
Pinal	1041	946	+92

6. Which county had the highest percentage of its filed cases completed in 2019?
    a. Maricopa
    b. Mohave
    c. Pima
    d. Pinal

Use the graph below to answer the question:

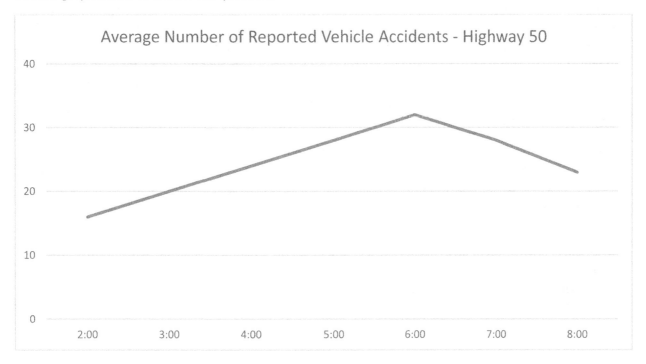

7. Which time below best represents the time that the number of vehicle accident reports start to decrease?
   a. 6:00
   b. 2:00
   c. 7:15
   d. 6:20

8. A woman is pulled over for swerving between lanes. Her papers are in order, but her speech is slurred, and she appears visibly very nervous. She was also driving 50 mph in a zone with a limit of 45 mph. Which of the following statutes would define this crime?
   a. The statute that prohibits driving while intoxicated
   b. The statute that requires all vehicles to be insured
   c. The statute that prohibits going over the designated speed limit
   d. The statute that prohibits suicide

9. Federal law has a statute that prohibits minors under twenty-one years of age from purchasing alcohol. Which of the following crimes can be defined using this statute?
   a. A man with gray hair and a long beard is found stealing beer from a convenience store.
   b. Gun shots were reportedly heard at a public park.
   c. There are reports of music being played too loud from an apartment late at night.
   d. A nightclub bouncer is reported to not be checking IDs before letting people enter the bar area.

Practice Test #1

10. OFFICER'S REPORT: I responded to a call about a missing eight-year-old child in Tempe, AZ, around midnight. When I arrived, a woman, calling herself Joan Fountain, identified herself as the mother of the lost child, James Fountain. She said the child usually never leaves the apartment complex, only going from his apartment to where his friend lives, but he has not been there and has not come back since the morning he was supposed to have left for school. He also will not answer his cell phone. She also says the school called and informed her he was absent from school that day. She seemed intoxicated and got irritated easily at my questions. Also, the child's bike was missing, and change was taken from a tray where the family kept loose coins.

Which of the following details in the report is NOT relevant to the case?
   a. The woman being intoxicated
   b. The missing bike and money
   c. The time of night
   d. The name of the mother

11. A man is discovered dead in his house, surrounded by drug paraphernalia and a half-empty bottle of liquor. Which of the following details in a case report would be the most relevant to the situation?
   a. The square footage of the house
   b. The type of shoes the man was wearing
   c. The type of drug paraphernalia found
   d. The number of officers present at the scene on arrival

12. An officer would MOST likely require backup in which of the following situations?
   a. There is a report of gang violence in a neighborhood.
   b. A young man is caught shoplifting from the grocery store.
   c. A man is accused of sexual assault at his workplace.
   d. A woman reports a missing purse containing very expensive jewelry.

13. An officer is MOST likely to ask an individual to step out of their car for inspection after pulling them over for which of the following?
   a. The driver has outdated insurance.
   b. There are five teenagers in the car with no adults present.
   c. The driver was speeding.
   d. There is a strong odor of alcohol on the driver's breath.

Use the following witness reports for questions 14 and 15.

> WITNESS REPORT 1: An elderly man I have never seen before came into the office just before noon and asked to speak privately with the boss and then, without waiting, just barged through the boss's door. About ten minutes later, I heard two gunshots, one right after the other, I think, or maybe a few minutes apart. When I went back into the office, both men were lying dead, and the gun was on the floor between them. Before the man entered the office, I asked my boss if he could come in first, of course, and he said sure. I didn't see him go in, though, but I was pretty busy, so I don't know.
>
> WITNESS REPORT 2: Raul, a middle-aged man who worked with us at the factory and who I spoke with in the mornings occasionally before work, told me that day he was going to see the boss about wages. He didn't sound upset, but you never know with Raul. He was a mysterious

102

Practice Test #1

fellow. I don't know when he went to the office because I didn't see him go, but I remember hearing the shots around noon because I was just about to go to lunch.

WITNESS REPORT 3: We were all about to go to lunch at noon when Raul, my partner on the factory line who comes to lunch with us every day, says he is skipping the day because he needs to speak with the boss. He had been there awhile, but he was only forty or so, not like us old timers who got on because of a whole government layoff thing. Sure, we were kind of upset about stuff here and there, but I don't think I heard him say anything really. He wouldn't talk to anyone but me about it too because it wasn't that serious and he was a private man. I mean I liked my boss. Sometimes he was mean or didn't treat us right, but he was just a man, I guess. I don't really talk about the company. I just do my work, and I don't talk to Raul really either.

WITNESS REPORT 4: I didn't really see it happen, but I knew it would. I never trust anyone in this company. They all just got hired because of some dirty government business. I didn't know or speak to Raul, or any of them, except I guess one morning we all kind of had a discussion, but I wasn't really involved, I swear! Don't question me anymore!

14. Which of the following details is most likely true?
    a. The shooting happened around noon.
    b. There was no discussion among workers that day.
    c. Raul is a very old man.
    d. Raul is shy.

15. Which witness is most likely telling the truth?
    a. Witness 1
    b. Witness 2
    c. Witness 3
    d. Witness 4

16. Alejandro, Jennifer, and Walt are competing in their track team's 500-meter dash. Jennifer finished behind Walt but ahead of Alejandro. Who won the race?
    a. Alejandro
    b. Jennifer
    c. Walt
    d. Not enough information

17. Which of the following is the next number in the series: 144, 133, 130, 119, 116...?
    a. 113
    b. 105
    c. 127
    d. 98

18. Three of the following words are similar, while one is different. Which one is different?
    a. Lake
    b. Ocean
    c. River
    d. Boat

19. Which of the following is the next number in the series: 288, 144, 72, 36, 18...?
   a. 4
   b. 12
   c. 6
   d. 9

20. On their driving test, Anna earned 97 points, which was 12 more points than Michael. Michael scored 10 points higher than Tom, who scored 6 points lower than Jaime. What was Tom's score?
   a. 109
   b. 22
   c. 75
   d. 91

Answer Explanations #1

Memorization

1. B

2. C

3. D

4. B

5. A

6. B

7. C

8. D

9. C

10. B

11. B

12. D

13. A

14. D

15. C

16. D

17. B

18. C

19. A

20. B

21. A: Route stops may have multiple names because they pass through multiple lines. Route A only passes through five stops because it travels along the straight B line even though the directions suggest that different lines are involved because of the intersections. Although Choice *D* has the simplest instructions, it will actually pass through more stops when counted.

22. A: Because the information in the question states that line C is closed, only Choices *A* and *B* can be used to reach the destination, Choices *C* and *D* both include the closed line. Choice *B* would pass through eight stops, one less than the number of stops of Choice *A*.

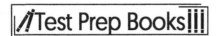

23. A: 32nd Street is the street that has the least amount of grey (traffic) that can reach the street with the accident. Choice *C*, taking 33rd Street, would be a delay, especially at the intersection by the accident. Choice *B*, 35th Street, is not listed on the map; and Choice *D*, taking Dumbar Street all the way to the accident, could also cause delays because most of the street is depicted as being grey.

24. B: Although Choice *C* would normally be the quickest route because it is a straight line to the destination, Central Street is depicted as being closed. Therefore, the next fastest route to take would be Choice *B* because there is less traffic than the other choices, and it will lead directly to the destination using the streets depicted on the map.

25. D: Uncommon features that may be unique to an individual will be the most helpful to take note of when recalling faces to match sketches and narrow down options. A birthmark on a face is easily recognizable and uncommon enough to help identify matching sketches. Choice *A*, hair length, and Choice *B*, a smiling face, can be easily changed or found on any number of people at a given time, and Choice *C*, the cigarette, could be left out of a drawing.

Written Comprehension

1. D: Based on the passage, the most accurate statement is that some court records are sealed for reasons such as protecting the privacy of a minor involved in the case. While many court records can be accessed in online databases, some must be requested from a specific department, such as the Appellate Court. The majority of court records are considered part of the public domain, but not all records are made public. Military status is part of court documents and can therefore be revealed through those records that are made part of the public domain.

2. A: Based on the passage, the most accurate statement is that each state makes its own laws about how and when court records can be accessed by the public. While a judge can seal a record for a minor, it is not required. Also, judges do have the power to seal a record, but this is usually only done in extraordinary circumstances. In California, only some court records are available through county databases. Appellate and Supreme Court records must be accessed through the Appellate Court.

3. D: Based on the passage, the new law discussed will add training in what to do at a traffic stop to driver's education courses in Illinois, so this is the best answer. The new law only adds this component to the courses; it does not require that all drivers take the course. The law does not target underage drivers; it aims to protect them from doing anything risky during a stop, so the goal is not to pull over more teens. While it is not advised that drivers reach under the seat or argue with the officer, it is not illegal. Drivers should know their rights and exercise them.

4. C: Based on the passage, the best answer is that traffic stop training is aimed to prevent drivers from panicking when they are pulled over. Traffic stops are actually one of the more dangerous parts of being a police officer. While a young driver may learn from a police officer during a traffic stop, the paragraph focuses more on how driver's education courses are being updated to instruct young drivers on how to handle a traffic stop. The paragraph is stressing a need for education in what to do during a traffic stop, so the last statement contradicts that point. A driver who believes he is driving safely could still be stopped.

5. D: Choice *D* is the most accurate because the passage states that 31 states allow private citizens to open carry a firearm without a license. Thus, open carry laws are not very strict in all 50 states. California, Florida, and Illinois are singled out not because they allow open carry without a permit, but

Answer Explanations #1

because they are the only states that prohibit open carry of a firearm. Because of these states' laws on open carry, Choice *C*'s statement about 19 states requiring a permit cannot be true.

6. C: This is the most accurate statement because the passage asserts that all states including the District of Columbia allow for concealed carry of a firearm in public. The passage states that forty-two states, not eight, require a permit for concealed carry of a firearm in public. The "may issue" law allows states to pose more restrictions on who can be granted a concealed carry permit, while the "shall issue" law is much less restrictive.

7. B: The passage begins by stating the Miranda rights have been required since the 1966 Supreme *Court case* of Miranda v. Arizona, so this is the most accurate statement. The Miranda rights do not require the person in custody to remain silent, but they do notify them that they may remain silent if they choose to. Police officers must read the Miranda rights to any person in custody to protect the information they may get in interrogation. The Miranda rights tell the person in custody that they have the right to an attorney and that one will be provided to them if they cannot afford an attorney.

8. C: This statement is the most accurate because the passage states that in order to comply with Miranda rights, a person in custody must waive their rights. Miranda rights protect both the person in custody and the police. They also protect the admissibility of the information gained in any questioning. While police officers could be sued for any number of reasons, the passage does not make any indication that they could be sued for not reading a person in custody their Miranda rights. When a person has not waived their Miranda rights, the information they provide may not be admissible in court.

9. B: The passage indicates that police departments can successfully use social media to identify suspects and find missing persons. The passage does not deter police departments from using any social media outlet. Trust can be built with the community when they feel they have a voice through police social media sites. The passage states that the use of social media by police departments is actually growing in popularity.

10. A: Based on the passage, this statement is the most accurate because it calls for a single point of contact to manage the sites for continuity. The passage actually calls for police departments to limit details on ongoing cases, but it does not say it is not beneficial in these cases. For example, the paragraph states that social media can be helpful in identifying a suspect, which would be for an ongoing case. That does not mean they should reveal all the details of the crime or anything that might jeopardize the case. While some departments may opt to hire a consultant to set up their social media sites, nothing in the paragraph suggests that this is necessary.

11. B: The correct answer is *B*. Cross-contamination has the potential to destroy any evidence collected and jeopardize any case a prosecutor may be hoping to build against a suspect. For that reason, it is one of the most important aspect of collecting evidence. Choice *A* is incorrect because failure to properly store evidence in an appropriate sealed container can result in damage to the evidence as well as, possibly, cross-contamination as well. Therefore, storage is equally important. Choice *C* is incorrect as while crime scene investigators play an important role, there is far more that goes into a successful prosecution that the collection of evidence. Choice *D* is incorrect as crime scene investigators are trained at determining what items at a crime scene are of evidentiary value. Collecting everything from a scene and then narrowing down what might be evidence would consume far too much time.

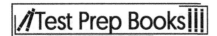

Answer Explanations #1

12. C: Choice C is correct. Monitoring the chain of custody is one of the essential elements of evidence collection as it ensures the integrity of the evidence. Choice A is incorrect as identifying a suspect comes after the crime scene investigation and once investigators have had a chance to gather and analyze the evidence. Choice B is incorrect. While avoiding cross-contamination is important, it is part of several steps (collection and storing) and not a step itself. Choice D is incorrect as it is not a step itself. Wearing gloves is important, but it is part of the collection process.

13. C: Choice C is correct. One of the goals of questioning a witness is to have them volunteer as much information as they possibly can and the best way to do that, without leading them, is to ask open ended questions. Choice A is incorrect. While open ended questions may create the opportunity to ask a follow-up, it's not the primary goal. Choice B is incorrect as open-ended questions may be effective on their own and not require a follow-up or close ended question. Choice D is incorrect as the goal is to not lead the witness to useful information. In fact, leading questions create reliability problems with the information provided and the information is not useful.

14. D: Choice D is correct. When preparing to interview witnesses at a crime or accident scene it is best to separate them to avoid them sharing their experiences. When they are not separated, they may talk about what they saw and that might change someone's story meaning you miss out on potentially important information. Choice A is incorrect. As noted, you don't want them sharing their stories as it may impact the stories they have to tell meaning you won't get a good picture of what happened. Different people will notice different things. Choice B is incorrect. While you do want to ask them open-ended questions, you want to separate them first. Overhearing another person's experience may taint someone's testimony. Choice C is incorrect. You want to make sure you gather evidence while it is fresh in their memory. This passage does not discuss letting them leave prior to gathering evidence.

15. B: Choice B is correct. The passage identifies both organization and clarity as the two most important elements of report writing. Choice A is incorrect. While details are important in the report, how they are organized is paramount. Choice C is incorrect. While concise is a great quality in good writing, it shouldn't come at the expense of other elements of the report, such as organization, clarity, and even including all the details and information. Choice D is incorrect. While organization is important, it may not be best to use the victim's timeline rather than a linear order of events as they happened. For example, a witness may have seen something prior to the victim which may change the organization and timeline.

16. D: Choice D is correct. Determining the timeline to use and the best way to present the events as they happened is a huge challenge. Multiple people may present multiple timelines and efforts to tell them all at once will impact clarity. Choice A is incorrect. The evidence can be reported at the end and is, therefore, not a challenge. Choice B is incorrect. While notetaking and remembering witness's recollections is important, it's not presented as a challenge here. Choice C is incorrect. While including relevant information and facts in the report is crucial, it's not noted as the biggest challenge in the passage. In fact, the passage notes that the end of the report presents an opportunity to include information which may be relevant.

17. A: Choice A is correct. According to the passage, the best time to include evidence that may not be included in witness reports is at the end of the report. Choice B is incorrect as evidence may be lost within the story and impact both organization and clarity. Choice C is incorrect as at the start, it may not be clear how information is related to the events or why something is evidentiary. Therefore, evidence should be included at the end, when its connection to the crime is, hopefully, clearer. Choice D is incorrect. While other reports regarding evidence may be required, evidence relevant to the crime should be included in the original report. The passage does not discuss additional reports.

18. A: Choice *A* is correct. The passage notes three reasons why someone might be nervous to testify and lack of control is one of those reasons. Choice *B* is incorrect. In fact, the passage notes that familiarizing oneself with the information and facts alleviates anxiety. Choice *C* is incorrect. While public speaking is easier with more experience, it's not noted in the passage nor is it clear that this is referencing experience public speaking vs. testifying. Choice *D* is incorrect. While that might have an impact on one's anxiety, it's not noted in the passage.

19. D: Choice *D* is correct. The passage notes a few ways to alleviate the anxiety and fear of testifying and reviewing the facts and laws is one great way. Choice *A* is incorrect. There is no mention of that in the passage, though there is mention that an attorney may research an officer. Choice *B* is incorrect. While that might be useful in familiarizing an officer with the experience, it's not noted in the passage. Choice *C* is incorrect. While practicing public speaking is a good tact, and might be inferred from the information given in the passage, it is not listed in the passage specifically as a step.

20. B: Choice *B* is correct. The last thing an officer should want is for a prosecutor to be caught off guard or to not be prepared for questions related to their personnel file. For that reason, officers should be open with those involved in the case, such as prosecutors, regarding any marks or reports that may be found in their personnel files. Choice *A* is incorrect. The prosecutor should have the facts of the case based on police and investigator reports. Choice C is incorrect. What an officer might have learned about an attorney or judge isn't particularly relevant, and it is likely other attorneys have access to the same information. Further, the passage doesn't discuss that solution. Choice *D* is incorrect. While revealing one's anxiety might be helpful and allow a prosecutor to help an officer prepare, it's not discussed in the passage.

Written Expression

1. C: disobedience

2. C: precinct

3. B: opportunity

4. D: accidentally

5. D: committed

6. B: *Stealing* and *embezzling* are synonyms.

Stealing: the act of taking a thing from somebody that isn't one's own

Embezzling: to defraud someone or to steal property (often money) entrusted into one's care

7. A: *Cleared* and *exonerated* are synonyms.

Cleared: to be absolved of misunderstanding or doubt

Exonerated: to be pronounced not guilty of criminal charges

Answer Explanations #1

8. C: *Death* and *fatality* are synonyms.

Death: the event of a person's life ending

Fatality: a death that occurs as the result of an accident, disaster, war, or disease

9. D: *Fake* and *forgery* are synonyms.

Fake: an imitation of reality; a simulation

Forgery: to create or imitate something (e.g., an object or document) with the intent to deceive others or profit from the sale of it

10. A: *Hidden* and *latent* are synonyms.

Hidden: something kept out of sight or concealed

Latent: a thing that's hidden, or something that exists but hasn't been developed yet

Reasoning

1. C: The next number in the series is 64. In this series, each successive number is 4 less than the number that preceded it. So, to find the next number in the series, subtract 4 from the previous number.

2. D: The next number in the series is 32. In this series, the numbers increase by one more with each successive number. So, there is an increase of 1 between the first two numbers, an increase of 2 between the second and third numbers, an increase of 3 between the third and fourth numbers, and an increase of 4 between the fourth and fifth numbers. The next number in the series should be 5 more than the last number given.

3. D: The correct answer is Matt, Andrew, Geeta. According to the prompt, Andrew watches more television than Geeta. Since the goal is to rank the friends in order of how much television they watch *from most to least*, the list should read the following way so far: Andrew, Geeta. The prompt goes on to say that Andrew watches less television than Matt, so Matt must be added to the list above Andrew.

4. A: The word *notebook* is not like the other three. A pencil, pen, and crayon can all be used to write or draw. A notebook is something that is written or drawn in, rendering it different from the other three words.

5. B: The next number in the series is 44. Beginning with the first number in the series, every other number increases by 1. Beginning with the second number, every other number decreases by 1. So, to find the next number in the series, decide which pattern the missing number should continue. The missing number should continue the increasing by 1 pattern started by the first number in the series. Looking only at that pattern, the series reads 41...42...43. Continuing that pattern, the missing number should be 44.

6. B: The needed information can be found by looking at each title on the chart. Only the county, the number of cases filed, and the cases completed are relevant to the question, meaning the Cases Completed Increase/Decrease From 2018 information is not needed. Then, by dividing the number of completed cases by the number of cases filed for each county, the percentage of completed cases can

Answer Explanations #1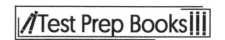

be found, proving that although Maricopa had the most cases, Mohave had the highest completion percentage (93 percent).

7. D: By following the labels on the graph, the time can be found by looking at the numbers at the bottom of the image. The numbers on the side of the graph represent the amount, increasing as they go upward. By identifying the point on the graph where the slope starts to decrease, the answer can be traced back to the time at the bottom. However, the highest point on the graph point lies right on the 6:00 p.m. time slot, meaning that the approximate time is between 6:00 and 6:30.

8. A: The crime that could possibly relate the most to this case, based on the driver's slurred speech and irresponsible driving, would be that she is intoxicated. It is described that her papers are in order, implying her insurance was up to date, making Choice B incorrect. Choice C is incorrect because even though the state law had regulated the speed limit in the area to 45 mph, the driver could not be considered to be speeding if she was only driving 5 mph over the limit. Choice D is also incorrect because there is no indication the driver is suicidal.

9. D: Although not explicitly stated in the scenario, the logical outcome will most likely result in the underage drinking of minors as defined by the statute. The remaining choices, although possible crimes in their own respect, still do not match the statute given because they cannot be related to the incident in a logical way.

10. A: Even though the mother's state of mind may be questionable, it does not relate to the case of the missing child and will do little to help solve the problem. Choice B, the information about the lost bike and money may lead to where the child may have gone, and Choice C, the time of night, and Choice D, the name of the mother, are important details to frame the background of the story.

11. C: Discovering what type of paraphernalia was possibly used could lead to a cause of death and is the only information relevant to the man's death. The remaining choices, although detailing information related to the scene, have no direct influence on the case of how the man died and do not provide insight on how the case can be solved.

12. A: Gang violence could involve multiple, dangerous individuals, so for the officer's protection it would be best to call for backup in this instance. Choice B, Choice C, and Choice D all are minor, non-violent crimes involving few people; therefore, they would not necessarily require an officer to call for backup assistance.

13. D: Only if the officer has very reasonable cause to further investigate an individual should they take such action. However, if the smell of alcohol is too strong for an officer not to miss, there is a just cause in asking the individual to step out of their car because they could possibly be intoxicated and cause harm to others while behind the wheel. Choice A, Choice B, and Choice C do not give enough evidence that the driver is suspicious of anything other than a minor traffic violation.

14. A: The fact that repeats itself most often in each of the witness's reports is that the shooting took place around the workers' lunchtime, which was noon. There is also little reason indicated as to why the witnesses would lie about the time. The remaining choices, although they may also be true, are not verified by the repeated accounts of the different witnesses.

15. B: The only witness who does not contradict some of their information or is not too emotionally involved in their details is witness 2 because they are able to give a clear, concise detailing of what they

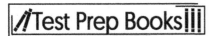

observed on the day of the crime. Their answers are given in an honest way that does not try to actively deny any events that took place in a defensive way.

16. D: Out of this group of three, Walt came in first. However, it's unclear who else on the team is participating in this race. Thus, there is insufficient information to determine whether or not Walt won the race.

17. B: The next number in the series is 105. In this series, the numbers are decreasing. The gap between each number alternates between 11 and 3. Following this pattern, the next number should be 11 less than the last number.

18. D: The word *boat* is not like the other three. A lake, ocean, and river are all bodies of water. A boat is a vessel used to traverse bodies of water, rendering it different from the other three words.

19. D: The next number in the series is 9. In this series, each successive number decreases by half.

20. C: Tom's score was 75. According to the prompt, Anna earned 97 points, which was 12 more than Michael. Michael earned 85 points, which is 10 more than Tom, which would give Tom 75 points.

Practice Test #2

Memorization

Examine the image below for one minute then remove it from view. You will then have a minute and a half to answer the questions that follow the image without referring back to the image. Do not read the questions during the image review period.

See questions on the next page.

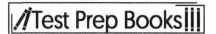

1. How many sheep were on the farm?
    a. 3
    b. 4
    c. 6
    d. 8

2. Which of the following is a task that was being completed on the farm?
    a. Feeding the horses
    b. Mowing the grass
    c. Milking the cows
    d. Splitting wood

3. How many horses were in the stable?
    a. 1
    b. 2
    c. 3
    d. 4

4. Which of the following animals were fenced in with the sheep?
    a. A dog
    b. Pigs
    c. Horses
    d. Donkey

5. How many people were working on the farm in total?
    a. 10
    b. 11
    c. 12
    d. 13

Practice Test #2

Directions for Questions 6-10:

Examine the image below for one minute then remove it from view. You will then have a minute and a half to answer the questions that follow the image without referring back to the image. Do not read the questions during the image review period.

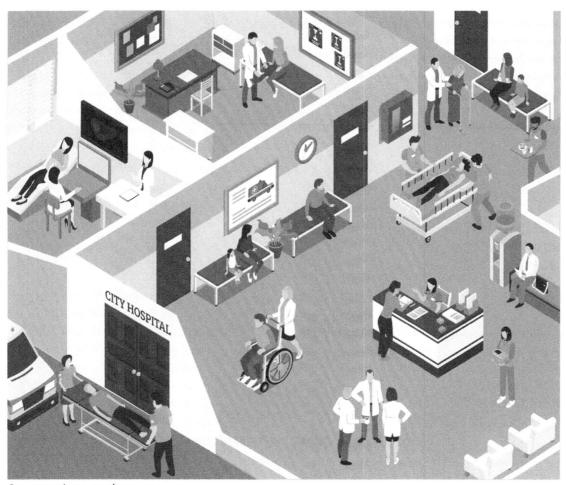

See questions on the next page.

6. How many doctors were talking to each other in the lobby?
   a. 2
   b. 3
   c. 4
   d. 5

7. What action was the doctor in the first room on the left performing?
   a. Helping a man on a stretcher
   b. Helping a woman with her walker
   c. Helping a woman with her ultrasound
   d. Helping a woman examine her knee

8. How many patients were on stretchers in the picture?
   a. 1
   b. 2
   c. 3
   d. 4

9. Roughly what was the time shown on the clock in the lobby?
   a. 12:10 PM
   b. 2:10 PM
   c. 4:00 PM
   d. 6:30 PM

10. What image was hanging on the wall in the waiting room?
    a. An ambulance
    b. An X-ray
    c. An ultrasound
    d. A medical cross

Written Comprehension

Read each passage and answer the related question:

In recent years, there has been much emphasis on police officers' use of body cameras while they are in the line of duty. These cameras provide a thorough visual and auditory record of all interactions between a police officer and the people with whom they interact while on the job, thereby creating an unbiased record of said interactions. Body cameras are an effective way to keep all parties honest in their reports of events. They limit the capacity for dishonesty from both police officers and laypeople, and they disincentivize officers from engaging in police misconduct. Footage from these cameras is always admissible in court as evidence. Body cameras effectively promote transparency in police work as well, thereby promoting public trust in law enforcement. However, there are certain situations in which the use of body cameras is not ethically permissible, such as when officers are interacting with minors or victims of sexual assault.

Practice Test #2

1. Based on the passage, what is one of the main reasons for the use of body cameras in law enforcement?
    a. They enable the officers to record their daily activities for personal review.
    b. They deter potential misconduct and can provide important evidence in court.
    c. They provide law enforcement officers with advanced surveillance capabilities.
    d. They allow the public to access live feeds of law enforcement operations.

In the United States, law enforcement agencies are not the only armed groups that can legally protect groups of people. Private security forces are non-governmental groups of people who provide protection services for hire. Their services often include guarding people and property, running security assessments, and guarding special events, whereas the police are primarily focused on apprehending criminals and enforcing laws. Private security groups are not legally required to work towards the collective good of a community; they often exclusively exist to serve the interests of the people and organizations who hire them. However, no matter how organized or well-armed private security forces are, they are comprised of citizens and therefore do not have nearly as much authority to exert over others as law enforcement does. For example, private security agents usually cannot make arrests, and they are never granted permission to search another person or their property without consent.

2. Based on the passage, how does the primary objective of private security differ from that of official law enforcement?
    a. Private security is tasked with enforcing laws, while law enforcement is primarily responsible for property protection.
    b. Private security focuses on defense against danger, while law enforcement focuses on apprehending criminals.
    c. Private security is primarily involved in the apprehension of criminals, while law enforcement concentrates on safeguarding property.
    d. Private security is primarily responsible for public safety, while law enforcement protects specific organizations or individuals.

The role that police play in immigration enforcement is heavily subject to change from area to area depending on the local laws in any given state or county. The United States Immigration and Customs Enforcement (ICE) is the federal institution in charge of immigration law, but state and local police forces can often have a smaller role to play in enforcing immigration law. This role varies heavily based on the jurisdiction and policies determined at the state or local levels. In some places, arrangements like the 278(g) program require officers to take on some degree of immigration enforcement duty, including probing suspected immigration breaches and initiating processes of deportation. However, there are also areas in the United States where law enforcement takes the opposite approach and seeks to provide sanctuary for immigrants rather than actively looking to enforce immigration law. In areas like this, local police may limit the degree to which they work with federal immigration officials, placing a higher priority on their community's sense of safety.

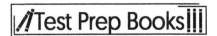

3. Based on the passage, what determines the extent of local law enforcement's role in immigration enforcement?
    a. The number of immigrants in the community
    b. The resources available to the police department
    c. The jurisdiction and local policies
    d. The overall crime rate in the area

Police are allowed to enlist the aid of others outside of designated law enforcement practices; this help can often come through an informant. Informants often have some sort of connection to the world of crime, and they can provide the police with unique intelligence regarding illegal activity and the people involved with it. Police can use informants to expand their information pool and gain access to places they normally could not go. However, using informants can lead to challenges and complications, such as determining the informant's trustworthiness. Informants can lie or bend the truth in ways that help them and their interests, so police must always take extra care when using this information, going the extra mile to validate any information they receive to see if it matches knowledge they already have.

4. Based on the passage, what is a primary challenge when using informants for investigations?
    a. Informants can manipulate information.
    b. Informants often refuse to work with law enforcement.
    c. Informants seldom have valuable information.
    d. Informants often compromise the integrity of investigations.

Hate crime laws deeply influence law enforcement operations in the United States, especially in recent years. These regulations seek to provide legal protections to people or groups who are attacked for belonging to marginalized races, faiths, genders, sexualities, or disability statuses. Police officers must be specially trained to spot hate crimes and enforce laws against them; such training requires familiarity with and understanding of these identities. There is, however, difficulty in identifying crimes as hate crimes since there must be reasonable evidence that the crime was driven by a source of prejudice. Because of this, investigations of hate crimes must be thorough. Not only should they include standard crime investigation steps (such as searching the crime scene, gathering evidence, and interviewing victims), but they should also inquiry into any past incidents that may show precedent for actions driven by prejudice.

5. Based on the passage, what most complicates the enforcement of hate crime legislation?
    a. The criteria for categorizing a crime as a hate crime
    b. The lack of adequate hate crime training for police officers
    c. The ambiguous definition of a hate crime
    d. The difficulty of prosecuting hate crimes due to lack of evidence

Police officers in the United States are a critical force in identifying, responding to, and dealing with hate crimes. When a hate crime is reported, the police are required to follow up swiftly. Officers must gather evidence, interview victims, and consider precedence. They also usually connect victims of hate crimes to resources that can provide additional support for recovery. Furthermore, police must extend this initiative into community outreach efforts. Police should encourage victims and witnesses of hate crimes to report them, thereby enabling law enforcement officers to foster a community that appropriately criminalizes hate crimes. To properly do this, police officers are given dedicated training to improve their understanding of hate crimes and the communities they impact the most.

6. Based on the passage, which of the following best describes the role of police officers in responding to hate crimes?
    a. They primarily focus on identifying and locating perpetrators.
    b. They conduct investigations, apprehend perpetrators, and engage in community outreach and victim support.
    c. They focus on public awareness—making the community aware of people who commit hate crimes—since such crimes are not punishable by law.
    d. They act as a support system for victims, offering counseling and emotional support.

In the United States, minors or juveniles (anyone under 18 years old) are protected by a specific set of laws in the juvenile justice system. These laws are similar to, but separate from, the laws that apply to adults. This separate system exists because minors may not fully grasp the legal system and the complications therein. Much like adults, juveniles are owed a due process, which includes, but is not limited to, the right to full knowledge of the charges against them, the right to a lawyer, the right to question witnesses, the right to remain silent to avoid incrimination, and the right to a trial presided over by an impartial judge. One thing that sets the juvenile justice system apart from the regular justice system is that juveniles do not always have the right to a trial by jury. Juvenile justice proceedings are also given greater privacy than regular proceedings, and punishments more often focus on rehabilitation than punishment.

7. Based on the passage, which of the following rights is NOT universally guaranteed for juveniles in the American criminal justice system?
    a. The right to confront and cross-examine witnesses
    b. The right to legal representation
    c. The right to be notified of the charges against them
    d. The right to a trial by jury

People who suffer from the effects of crime have certain rights and privileges in the law enforcement system that allow them a degree of fair involvement in the prosecution of the offending criminal. Most importantly, victims have the right to know about all primary proceedings of the ongoing case, which lets them stay informed and take part if or when they want to. When a court hearing occurs that impacts a victim, they are given the opportunity (but are not forced) to express their perspective through a victim impact statement, thereby allowing their experiences to be recognized in a court of law. Often, victims can receive restitution in cases where they were harmed or otherwise wronged; this means that if the offender is found guilty, the victim may be owed a sum of money from the offender that corresponds to the loss or harm inflicted. Lastly, victims are thoroughly protected from threats and harm throughout the entirety of the case.

8. Based on the passage, which of the following is NOT a right conferred to victims within the criminal justice system?
   a. The right to be informed about significant case proceedings
   b. The right to give victim impact statements
   c. The right to protection during the case
   d. The right to impact the sentencing of the convicted perpetrator

The legality of stop-and-frisk practices by police officers traces back to *Terry v. Ohio* (1968), a Supreme Court case that ruled that an officer can search a person for weapons if the officer has a solid reason based on provable facts to believe that the person in question is engaged in a specific crime and/or may be carrying a weapon. The aim of the ruling was to ensure the safety of police officers, but the ruling has stirred up much controversy regarding its interactions with the Fourth Amendment, which grants citizens protection against unwarranted search and seizure. To prevent stop-and-frisk tactics from being used incorrectly or disproportionately, it is crucial that police departments emphasize that stop-and-frisk practices must be used in a legitimate and unbiased manner.

9. Based on the passage, at what point is the application of stop-and-frisk tactics deemed legal?
   a. When an officer has a reasonable, fact-based suspicion that a person may be involved in criminal activity and could be armed
   b. When an officer believes that a person is acting suspiciously
   c. When the entire law enforcement agency holds suspicion about a person's possible involvement in criminal activities
   d. When an officer feels threatened

Forensic science exists at the intersection between science and law enforcement; it utilizes scientific tools and techniques to analyze evidence and inform the actions of law enforcement officers. Forensic sciences utilize a wide array of scientific fields, including biology, chemistry, physics, and psychology. Forensic scientists attempt to fill in as much as they can about the story of a crime by analyzing the gathered evidence, be it DNA, fingerprints, weapons, camera footage, or digital data. DNA specifically has recently skyrocketed in usefulness, resulting in a much higher number of accurate crime investigations. Also worth noting is the recent spike in digital forensics, which responds to the ever-growing threat of cybercrime. Digital forensics departments can analyze computer systems to determine how cybercrimes occurred or extract valuable information from digital devices like smartphones and tablets, which goes a long way in punishing and preventing crimes like hacking or online fraud.

10. Based on the passage, which of the following types of evidence is NOT typically analyzed in forensics?
    a. Blood samples
    b. Written correspondences
    c. Fingerprints
    d. Digital data

Practice Test #2

Written Expression

Directions: In the following sentences, choose the correct spelling of the missing word. Mark the letter that identifies your choice on the answer sheet.

1. When in need of advice on a case, I consult with my _____.
   a. sergeant
   b. sergant
   c. saergant
   d. seargeant

2. The car was _____ new when she purchased it.
   a. practicilly
   b. practicaly
   c. practikally
   d. practically

3. The suspect fled the _____ on foot.
   a. seen
   b. scene
   c. sceen
   d. sene

4. The fugitive was _____ only a few blocks from his home.
   a. apprehanded
   b. aprended
   c. apprehended
   d. aprehended

5. The new officer has high hopes to one day be promoted all the way to _____.
   a. captain
   b. captin
   c. captian
   d. captan

Directions: Read each sentence carefully and select the answer that is closest in meaning to the underlined word. Use prefix/suffix definitions and context clues to help eliminate incorrect answers.

6. The officer was held responsible for <u>deviating</u> from protocol.
   a. Following
   b. Differing
   c. Consenting
   d. Ignoring

7. The officer felt <u>provoked</u> by the suspect's accusations.
   a. Instigated
   b. Humiliated
   c. Scorned
   d. Insulted

8. The officers responded to a noise <u>ordinance</u> complaint.
   a. Law
   b. Guideline
   c. Direction
   d. Amplification

9. The captain knew exactly where his <u>jurisdiction</u> began and ended.
   a. Experience
   b. Authority
   c. Compromises
   d. Orders

10. The suspect <u>insisted</u> that he'd been framed.
    a. Demanded
    b. Explained
    c. Maintained
    d. Admitted

Reasoning

1. A man is running down the street carrying a bag and pulling off a mask. What has most likely happened?
   a. A murder has occurred.
   b. A store was robbed.
   c. A car accident has occurred.
   d. A marathon has started.

2. A witness to a murder says that the suspect was a Caucasian male approximately six feet tall, of slight build and had a mustache. Additionally, the suspect was wearing a black leather jacket and responded to someone saying, "Paul, get in the car!" Which was the LEAST useful piece of information given by the witness?
   a. The suspect was a Caucasian male
   b. The suspect responded to the name Paul
   c. The suspect had a mustache
   d. The suspect wore a black leather jacket

3. A woman reports that she was assaulted while walking home. She says that she had gone to a bar with some friends, and after her friends left the bar with dates, she walked home alone. What was the first event in her story?
   a. She was assaulted.
   b. She went to a bar.
   c. Her friends left the bar.
   d. She walked home alone.

Practice Test #2

4. A group of teenagers has gathered at a bus stop and are being considerably loud. Upon examination, it appears that two of them are fighting. What would be the MOST appropriate response to the situation?
   a. Approach the group and de-escalate the situation.
   b. Fire a warning shot.
   c. Call for backup.
   d. Fire tear gas into the gathering.

5. An officer arrives at the scene of a domestic violence call. The husband answers the door with a bloody nose and his wife can be heard in the background screaming at him. What would be the best first step in this situation?
   a. Arrest the husband right away.
   b. Enter the domicile armed.
   c. Separate the couple and get statements.
   d. Contact a women's domestic violence shelter.

6. Choose the sequence of numbers that is in the correct order from smallest to largest.
   a. -3, 0, -1, 4
   b. -7, -3, 5, 2
   c. -4, -1, 3, 7
   d. 4, 1, -2, -5

7. Jane is four years older than Billy, who is twice the age of Samantha. If Samantha will turn 20 years old in three months, how old will Jane be six years from now?
   a. 44
   b. 46
   c. 48
   d. 50

8. Which of the following shapes is least like the others?
   a. Oval
   b. Rectangle
   c. Trapezoid
   d. Square

9. Which of the following is the next letter in the sequence: B, D, F, H, J...?
   a. K
   b. L
   c. M
   d. N

10. John and Jane Smith have two children, Todd and Sarah. If Todd and Sarah each have two children, and each of Todd and Sarah's children have three children, then how many grandchildren do John and Jane have?
    a. 2
    b. 4
    c. 12
    d. 24

11. Name the missing number in the sequence: 1, 1, 2, 3, 5, ___, 13, 21, 34.
    a. 5
    b. 6
    c. 7
    d. 8

The next question is based upon the following graph:

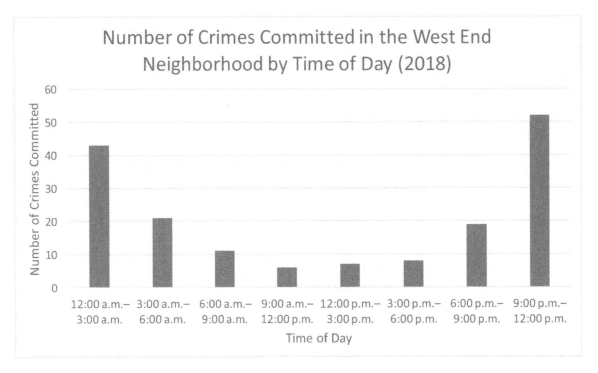

12. Based on the above data, during which eight-hour shift should an officer patrol the West End neighborhood?
    a. 12:00 a.m.–8:00 a.m.
    b. 8:00 a.m.–4:00 p.m.
    c. 12:00 p.m.–8:00 p.m.
    d. 8:00 p.m.–4:00 a.m.

The next question is based upon the following graphs:

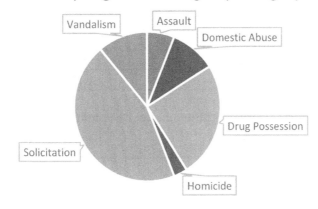

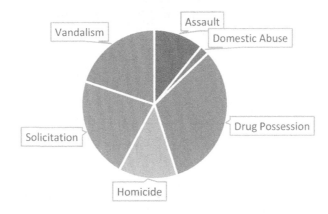

13. Which is most accurate based on the above information on the two boroughs?
    a. Fairview Borough would benefit less than Springfield Borough from an undercover drug program.
    b. Fairview Borough would benefit more than Springfield Borough from a domestic abuse education program.
    c. Springfield Borough would benefit more than Fairview Borough from a gun buyback program.
    d. Springfield Borough would benefit more than Fairview Borough from an undercover prostitution operation.

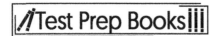

The next question is based upon the following table:

Annual Number of Violent Crimes per 100,000 Residents		
City	2015	2021
Lawrence	910	950
Lowell	780	795
Manchester	205	290
Plattsburg	210	170

14. Which city had the greatest increase in the number of violent crimes from 2015 to 2021?
   a. Lawrence
   b. Lowell
   c. Manchester
   d. Plattsburg

The next question is based upon the following table:

Percent Change in Offenses 2022-2023					
Township	Violent crime	Murder	Rape	Robbery	Aggravated Assault
Total	-5.6	-11.1	-4.2	-6.7	-12.5
Canton	-7.3	-14.4	-5.7	-11.5	-15.5
Main	-7.2	-12.7	-6.4	-5.0	-13.8
Polk	-4.0	-10.5	-2.7	-1.4	-10.3
Spring	-6.2	-10.1	-4.2	-11.3	-12.7

15. Which Township saw the greatest decrease in violent crime from 2022 to 2023?
   a. Canton
   b. Main
   c. Polk
   d. Spring

16. An officer encounters a vehicle parked in a local park after dark. Upon approaching, he sees that there are people inside. The older man behind the wheel says he is on a date with his girlfriend. The officer notices that the female in the passenger seat is noticeably younger. Her shirt is torn, and she appears to have been crying. What is the most appropriate course of action?
   a. Arrest the man on suspicion of rape.
   b. Ask the passenger to exit the vehicle and ask her if she's okay.
   c. Cite the man for trespassing and tell the couple to move on.
   d. Tell the couple to continue their date elsewhere.

17. OFFICER NOTES: December 23, 2021, around 10:30 p.m., arrived at 132 E. 20th Ave. in Montgomery, AL. Spoke with John Chapman, identified as property owner, regarding a forced entry and items missing from inside the home.

Which of the following options most clearly and accurately presents the facts from the report above?
   a. After receiving a call about forced entry and burglary from a home in Montgomery, AL, I drove to the home of John Chapman at 132 20th Ave at about 10:30 p.m.
   b. At 10:30 p.m. on December 23, 2021, I responded to a call at 132 20th Ave. Upon arrival, I spoke with the property owner, John Chapman. Mr. Chapman had arrived home to find that someone had forced entry into his home and taken several items.
   c. I arrived at the home of John Chapman at 10:30 p.m. on December 23, 2021. He said he was missing his Xbox and a watch. He lives at 132 E. 20th Ave in Montgomery, AL.
   d. I responded to a report of burglary at the home of John Chapman on December 23.

18. If a person is facing north and then rotates 270 degrees to the left, which direction will they be facing after the rotation?
   a. North
   b. South
   c. East
   d. West

19. If all basketball players are taller than six feet, and Alex and Pat are both basketball players, what is the logical conclusion?
   a. Alex and Pat are over six feet tall.
   b. Alex is taller than Pat.
   c. Pat is taller than Alex.
   d. Alex and Pat both like playing basketball.

20. Michael weighs 167 pounds. Jill weighs 142 pounds. Alice weighs 125 pounds. Scott weighs less than Jill, but more than Alice. What is a possible weight for Scott?
   a. 120 pounds
   b. 135 pounds
   c. 150 pounds
   d. 165 pounds

Answer Explanations #2

Memorization

1. C: There are 6 sheep on the farm.

2. D: There is a man chopping wood on the farm.

3. B: There are 2 horses in the stable.

4. A: There is 1 dog in the fenced area with the sheep. There are also cows, but that was not an answer choice.

5. C: There are 12 people in total working on the farm.

6. B: There are 3 doctors talking with each other in the lobby.

7. C: In the first room on the left, an ultrasound is taking place.

8. B: There are 2 patients shown in the picture that are on stretchers.

9. A: The clock in the lobby is showing roughly 12:10 PM.

10. A: There is an image of an ambulance in the waiting room.

Written Comprehension

1. B: Choice *B* is correct because the passage states that body cameras are helpful both in deterring misconduct and in utilizing footage as evidence. Choice *A* is incorrect because the passage does not mention personal review of body camera footage. Choice *C* is incorrect because the passage does not discuss body cameras being used for surveillance purposes. Choice *D* is incorrect because the passage does not mention the public getting access to body camera footage.

2. B: Choice *B* is correct because private security primarily protects people and things, thereby deterring danger, while the primary focus of law enforcement is on enforcing laws and apprehending criminals. Choices *A*, *C*, and *D* are all incorrect because they reverse the roles of the two entities.

3. C: Choice *C* is correct because the passage lists state and local jurisdiction and policies as factors that determine the police's role in immigration law enforcement. Choices *A*, *B*, and *D* are not discussed in the passage.

4. A: Choice *A* is correct because the text mentions reliability as a major concern when working with informants, stating that they can alter the information to better serve their own interests. Choice *B* is incorrect because, in the case of police investigations, informants do work with the police. Choice *C* is incorrect because informants would not be used if their information was not valuable. Choice *D* is incorrect because the passage does not mention that informants could compromise an investigation's integrity; it only mentions that their information could be dubious.

5. A: Choice *A* is correct because the passage explains how the primary difficulty of hate crime legislation is establishing a motive based on prejudice. Choice *B* is incorrect because officers are

Answer Explanations #2

generally trained to deal with hate crimes. Choice C is incorrect because the definition of a hate crime is not ambiguous. Choice D is incorrect because the passage does not list evidence gathering as a specific difficulty.

6. B: Choice B is correct because it lists every role of a police officer in combatting hate crimes as described in the passage. Choice A is incorrect because identification and location is only a small part of apprehending people who commit hate crimes. Choice C is incorrect because police have full authority to punish hate crimes. Choice D is incorrect because the police are tasked with connecting victims to support systems; they are not the support systems themselves.

7. D: Choice D is correct because the passage mentions that the right to a trial by jury is not always guaranteed to juveniles. Choices A, B, and C are incorrect because the text clearly states that juveniles have these rights.

8. D: Choice D is correct because the passage does not mention that victims have the right to influence their offender's sentence in any way. However, they do have the right to be informed, heard, and protected during the trial. Therefore, Choices A, B, and C are incorrect.

9. A: Choice A is correct because the passage states that stop-and-frisk tactics are only allowed when a police officer has a fact-based reason to suspect that the person in question is involved in criminal activity and may be armed. Choice B is incorrect because suspicion without basis in fact is not enough to justify stop-and-frisk. Choice C is incorrect because an agency-wide suspicion is still not enough without provable facts to support it. Choice D is incorrect because a subjective feeling of being threatened is not enough without specific, fact-based suspicion of criminal activity.

10. B: Choice B is correct because forensic science deals with the scientific aspects of evidence, and general written correspondence falls under the jurisdiction of general law enforcement investigators. Evidence like blood samples (Choice A), fingerprints (Choice C), and digital data (Choice D) all fall under the purview of forensic science.

Written Expression

1. A: sergeant

2. D: practically

3. B: scene

4. C: apprehended

5. A: captain

6. B: *Deviating* is used in this context as a verb to indicate the officer's actions. The officer was held responsible—as in disciplined—for *differing* from regulation. The officer would not have been disciplined for *following* or *consenting* to regulations. While the officer might have been disciplined for *ignoring* regulations, *ignoring* does not have the same meaning as *deviating*, which means to go against something.

7. A: In this sentence, *provoked* indicates that the officer was led to act. Choice *A*, *instigated*, also indicates that the officer was led to act. While the officer may have felt *humiliated*, *scorned*, or *insulted* by the suspect's accusations, none of these words indicate that the officer was motivated to take action.

8. A: *Ordinance* is used in this context as a noun to indicate a *law*. Like a *law*, an *ordinance* must be obeyed. Neither *guideline* nor *direction* convey the same meaning as *law*, since they do not carry the same connotation. *Amplification*, which indicates increased frequency, is irrelevant in this context.

9. B: *Jurisdiction* indicates the scope of one's *authority*. To know where one's *experience*, *compromises*, and *orders* begins and ends is not the same as knowing where one's *authority* begins and ends. A knowledge of one's *authority* indicates knowing the contexts in which one has license to act.

10. C: *Insisted* is used in this context as the past tense form of a verb that means to contend, uphold, or claim. Choice *C*, *maintained*, fits this meaning because it conveys that the suspect contended, upheld, and claimed their own innocence. Neither *demanded* nor *explained* fits the context because the former would imply that the suspect was able to make demands and the latter would imply that the suspect provided proof or evidence of his or her innocence. *Admitted*, which means confessed, misses the context of the sentence.

Reasoning

1. B: Choice *B* is correct given that that is removing a mask that could have been used as a disguise and is carrying a bag that could be holding cash, robbery is the most explanation. Choice *A* is incorrect because there is no corpse, which would be evidence of a murder. Choice *C* is incorrect because there was no evidence of an accident, such as a disabled vehicle or the sounds of a collision. Choice *D* is incorrect because, although a running man could be evidence of a marathon, the fact that he is carrying a bag and pulling off a mask would suggest that he is not in a marathon, as marathon runners do not carry bags or wear masks while running.

2. D: Choice *D* is correct because the suspect could have taken the jacket off or gotten rid of it, making it less important in finding him. Choices *A* and *B* are incorrect because knowing that the suspect is a Caucasian male that responds to the name Paul is very useful information in finding the suspect. Choice *C* is incorrect because the suspect could have shaved his mustache or removed a fake mustache; however, this is slightly less likely than removing his black leather jacket, so this information is slightly more useful than Choice *D*.

3. B: Choice *B* is correct because going to the bar was the first event in the woman's story. Choices *A*, *C*, and *D* are incorrect because these events happened after she went to the bar.

4. A: Choice *A* is correct because this is clearly a tense situation, but it's one that might easily be handled by the mere presence of police. Further action could take place as appropriate. Choices *B* and *D* are incorrect because they are excessive uses of force that could also hurt innocent bystanders. Choice *C* is incorrect because backup does not need to be called unless the situation escalates and the officer needs help.

5. C: Choice *C* is correct because it is a good idea to separate this couple right away to minimize further harm and get statements to try to determine what has happened. Choices *A* and *D* are incorrect because the officer doesn't have enough information yet to make an arrest. Choice *B* is incorrect because it is a far too aggressive move, which could escalate the situation.

Answer Explanations #2

6. C: Choice *C* is correct because -4 is less than -1, which is less than 3, which is less than 7. Choices *A* and *B* are incorrect because these sequences go from smaller to larger and then back to smaller. Choice *D* is incorrect because this sequence goes from largest to smallest.

7. C: Choice *C* is correct because Jane will be 48 years old in six years. The reasoning goes like this: If Samantha turns 20 years old in three months, that means that she is 19 years now. If Billy is twice the age of Samantha, that means that he is 38 years old. If Jane is four years older than Billy, that means that she is 42 years old now and will be 48 years old in six years.

8. A: Choice *A* is correct because an oval is a round shape, and all the other answer choices describe four-sided shapes. Choices *B*, *C*, and *D* are incorrect because each of them name shapes with four distinct sides.

9. B: The next letter in the sequence is the letter L because the series skips every other letter after starting with the letter B. Choice *A* is incorrect because it doesn't skip a letter, while Choices *C* and *D* are incorrect because they skip too many letters.

10. B: Choice *B* is correct because John and Jane have four grandchildren: Todd's two children and Sarah's two children. Choice *A* is incorrect because that is the number of children John and Jane have, not grandchildren. Choice *C* is incorrect because that is the number of great-grandchildren that John and Jane would have. Choice *D* is incorrect because that would be twice the amount of John and Jane's great-grandchildren.

11. D: Choice *D* is correct because in this sequence, each number is the sum of the previous two numbers. The missing number in the sequence is 8 because it is the sum of 3 and 5, the two previous numbers. Additionally, the sum of 5 and 8 is 13, which is the next shown number in the sequence. This sequence of numbers is known as the Fibonacci sequence, named after the 13th century Italian mathematician Fibonacci. Choices *A*, *B*, and *C* are incorrect because they do not fit this pattern.

12. D: This time period includes the two periods (9:00–12:00 a.m. and 12:00–3:00am) during which more crimes are committed than in any of the other time periods provided. Choices *A*, *B*, and *C* all include time periods with fewer crimes committed than during the time period given in Choice *A*.

13. D: The largest section of the upper pie chart for Springfield Borough is solicitation, which means prostitution is its primary crime. Choice *A* is incorrect because drug possession represents a greater proportion of the crime in Fairview Borough compared to Springfield Borough. Choice *B* is incorrect because domestic abuse represents a greater proportion of the crime in Springfield Borough compared to Fairview Borough. Choice *C* is incorrect because the crime most likely associated with guns (homicide) represents a greater proportion of the crime in Fairview Borough compared to Springfield Borough.

14. C: Crime in Manchester increased from 205 to 290, which is a +85 increase. Choice *A* is incorrect because crimes in Lawrence increased by 40. Choice *B* is incorrect because crimes in Lowell increased by 15. Choice *D* is incorrect because Plattsburg crimes decreased by 40.

15. A: Violent crime in Canton Township changed by -7.3%, which is a 7.3% decrease, the largest of the Townships listed. Choice *B* is incorrect because violent crime in Main Township decreased by 7.2%. Choice *C* is incorrect because violent crime in Polk Township decreased by 4.0%. Choice *D* is incorrect because violent crime in Spring Township decreased by 6.2%.

16. B: The woman's clothing and emotional state suggest she may have been assaulted. By inviting her out of the car, she may be more likely to tell an officer if she feels threatened or endangered. Choice *A* is

incorrect because the passage does not include enough evidence to give probable cause that rape has occurred. Choices C and D are not the best courses of action because they do not address the possibility that, based on the woman's appearance, an assault or other crime may have occurred in the car.

17. B: This choice presents the most relevant information from the notes in the most logical order. Choice A omits details and is not organized as clearly. Choice C includes unnecessary details and is not presented as clearly. Choice D is severely lacking in details.

18. C: Choice C is correct because person initially facing north would be facing east after rotating to the left (counter-clockwise) by 270 degrees, or three fourths of a full rotation. Choice A is incorrect because that would require a full 360-degree rotation. Choice B is incorrect because that would require a half-rotation of 180 degrees. Choice D is incorrect because that would require a 90-degree rotation (or a 270-degree rotation in the opposite direction).

19. A: Choice A is correct because if Alex and Pat both play basketball and all basketball players are over six feet tall, then Alex and Pat must also be over six feet tall. Choices B and C are incorrect because no information is given about either Alex's or Pat's specific height, so it is unknown which of the two is taller. Choice D is incorrect because, although both Alex and Pat play basketball, it isn't necessarily true that either of them enjoys it.

20. B: Choice B is correct because Scott must weigh between 125 pounds (Alice's weight) and 142 pounds (Jill's weight). Choice A is incorrect because it is less than Alice's weight of 125 pounds. Choices C and D are incorrect because they are more than Jill's weight of 142 pounds.

Practice Test #3

Memorization

Directions for Questions 1-5:

Examine the image below for one minute then remove it from view. You will then have a minute and a half to answer the questions that follow the image without referring back to the image. Do not read the questions during the image review period.

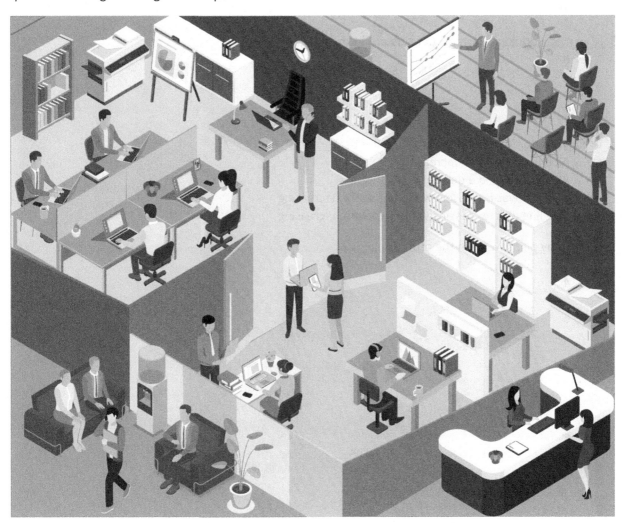

See questions on the next page.

133

Practice Test #3

1. How many laptops are pictured in the image?
    a. 7
    b. 8
    c. 9
    d. 10

2. How many people are standing in the image?
    a. 7
    b. 8
    c. 9
    d. 10

3. How many drinking water dispensers are in the image?
    a. 0
    b. 1
    c. 2
    d. 3

4. What were the results on the graph in the background?
    a. All lines showed an increase.
    b. All lines showed a decrease.
    c. One line was increasing while two were decreasing.
    d. One line was decreasing while two were increasing.

5. How many plants were in the office building?
    a. 3
    b. 4
    c. 5
    d. 6

Practice Test #3

Directions for Questions 6-10:

Examine the image below for one minute then remove it from view. You will then have a minute and a half to answer the questions that follow the image without referring back to the image. Do not read the questions during the image review period.

See questions on the next page.

6. Which of the following items were being sold in the park?
   a. Cotton Candy
   b. Pop Corn
   c. Lemonade
   d. Soda Pop

7. Which of the following activities were children participating in at the park?
   a. Spinning in chairs
   b. Climbing monkey bars
   c. Playing ball
   d. Hanging upside down

8. Which of the following was in the picture?
   a. Trampoline
   b. Swing set
   c. Pool
   d. Lemonade stand

9. How many buckets of popcorn were on the counter at the popcorn stand?
   a. 2
   b. 3
   c. 4
   d. 5

10. How many people were sitting, either on a bench or at a table?
    a. 3
    b. 4
    c. 5
    d. 6

Written Comprehension

Read each passage and answer the related question:

K-9 officers are specially trained police officers that handle police dogs. Officers are typically required to have three to five years of patrol experience before applying to a K-9 position. In addition to their traditional training, K-9 officers are required to complete several weeks of official K-9 training to be certified. This training includes skills such as drug and explosive detection, dog handling, crowd control, and search and rescue techniques. Most police dogs live and work with their handlers, so a K-9 officer will be expected to care for their dog full time. Most police dogs have 10-year careers, so this is a long-term commitment between dog and officer.

1. Which of the following statements best identifies the main idea of the preceding passage?
   a. Police dogs live and work with their handlers.
   b. K-9 officers should be prepared for a long-term commitment when they apply for this position.
   c. There are several requirements to becoming a K-9 officer.
   d. Patrol experience is necessary to apply for a K-9 officer position.

The Americans with Disabilities Act (ADA) was passed in 1990 to prohibit discrimination and to grant equal opportunity to those with disabilities in employment, transportation, communication, education, government services, and access to public places. In 2008, the ADA was amended to include a broader definition of the term "disability." Those who have physical or mental impairments that limit their lives in one or more major aspects can be considered disabled. This includes, but is not limited to, vision, speech, and hearing impairments, paralysis, intellectual disabilities such as cognitive impairment, mental illness, and chronic conditions such as epilepsy or multiple sclerosis. Temporary or naturally occurring conditions such as a broken limb, pregnancy, or the flu are not considered disabilities under this act.

2. Which of the following statements best defines the term *disability*?
    a. A physical or mental impairment that limits a major aspect of life.
    b. Vision, speech, and hearing impairments that prevent a person from working.
    c. Any illness that prevents a person from completing their daily tasks, such as the flu.
    d. Mental illnesses such as depression, anxiety, schizophrenia, and bipolar disorder.

Police officers cannot do their jobs to the fullest extent without building strong relationships with their communities, even beyond the tenets of community-oriented policing. People in said communities are less likely to communicate with law enforcement when they do not trust their police officers. When trust is present, however, communities are more likely to cooperate meaningfully with law enforcement by communicating problems and reporting crimes more frequently. Police can cultivate trust by engaging in community outreach programs and participating in existing community activities, which can often provide low-risk opportunities for communities to work together with their law enforcement officers. Police can also develop trust with their communities by offering regular and transparent communications about their operations and decisions. Clear and consistent communication tends to make communities feel more connected to their police force and therefore safer.

3. Based on the passage, why is community trust important in law enforcement?
    a. To discourage community members from reporting crimes to the police
    b. To enable law enforcement officers to act without accountability
    c. To limit the reach of law enforcement agencies
    d. To enhance cooperation and communication within the community

The rise of social media has changed the public-facing nature of policing, making it simultaneously simpler and more difficult. Some positive aspects of social media include its abilities to aid officers as they interact with the community and conduct investigations. Social media sites allow for immediate and open discussions between law enforcement officers and their communities, which can potentially offer valuable information and reinforce transparency and trust between the police and the public. However, social media also comes with difficulties, including the potential for false information to spread more quickly than it can be contained. This can lead to many complications, including undue public unease and interference with investigations. Furthermore, officers' online presence can potentially threaten their personal privacy and safety. Police departments must balance these potential risks and benefits to use social media optimally.

4. Based on the passage, how can social media benefit police officers?
    a. It ensures the personal safety of police officers.
    b. It provides a platform for offenders to be easily identified and tracked.
    c. It eliminates the possibility of misinformation during investigations.
    d. It allows for transparent communication, fostering trust between the police and the public.

    According to the exclusionary rule, a clause closely related to due process, evidence obtained through the violation of someone's constitutional rights (such as the right to privacy and protection against unreasonable search and seizure guaranteed by the Fourth Amendment) is not admissible in a court of law. In essence, illegally gathered evidence can't be used against someone. This rule is paramount to the retention of police integrity in the United States. It exists primarily to dissuade and disincentivize law enforcement officers from reaching beyond their legal protocols to gather evidence, thereby protecting people against potential police misconduct and maintaining the legal system's integrity. There is, however, an interesting exception to the rule. Coined as the "good faith" exception and established in *United States v. Leon* (1984), the exception holds that evidence seized under an invalid warrant that the acting officer reasonably assumed was valid can be admitted in a court of law.

5. Based on the passage, how does the exclusionary rule protect people from potential police misconduct?
    a. It temporarily decreases individuals' rights so that officers may legally obtain evidence.
    b. It permits law enforcement officers to gather evidence using any means necessary.
    c. It discourages law enforcement officers from overstepping their boundaries.
    d. It allows the use of any and all gathered evidence in court to ensure that criminals are more appropriately punished.

    Simply put, probable cause is the logical belief (based on facts and provable situations) that a crime has happened, is happening, or is about to happen. In order for probable cause to be actionable in the granting of a search warrant, it must also connect the stated crime with a person or place. Therefore, probable cause must be constantly considered by law enforcement with respect to investigations and searches. Probable cause is not to be confused with reasonable suspicion, which is another term used by law enforcement to justify police action. Reasonable suspicion is much less stringent in its requirement for proof than probable cause, and the rights it grants police officers are proportionally less. Reasonable suspicion can allow police to briefly detain someone, but it does not grant the rights to a search or to make an arrest. Courts tend to consider a wide array of circumstances and facts before confirming the existence of probable cause, whereas reasonable suspicion can be determined by law enforcement alone.

6. Based on the passage, probable cause is most heavily considered before issuing which of the following?
    a. Search warrants
    b. Firearms
    c. Arrest warrants
    d. Probation orders

    Police officers have a certain amount of leeway that allows them to make independent decisions based on the unique circumstances that occur in the line of duty. This leeway is referred to as police discretion, and it is one of many hotly debated topics surrounding law enforcement in the United States. Police discretion allows officers to adjust their actions fluidly based on the situations they face in the field, and it is the primary means by which officers utilize their professional judgement. When used legally and ethically, police discretion can make policing and police resource allocation more effective and efficient. However, police officers must uphold high standards of legality and ethics when exercising their discretion, lest irrational decision-making lead to improper law enforcement practices (such as excessive use of force or general police misconduct). Abuse of authority often leads directly to public mistrust. The way in which police officers handle their discretion is often the subject of public scrutiny.

7. Based on the passage, what is the primary risk associated with police discretion?
    a. It can lead to arbitrary decision-making if not exercised with high legal and ethical standards.
    b. It could result in inefficient law enforcement operations due to the flexibility involved.
    c. It causes a decrease in public trust due to the inherent authority it grants law enforcement officers.
    d. It could negatively impact the ability of officers to optimally allocate resources.

    The Fourth Amendment prohibits the government from conducting unlawful searches and seizures on citizens. Typically, a search and seizure is only lawful when paired with a legally obtained search warrant, which can be acquired through clearly established probable cause, though several exceptions do apply. These exceptions have been interpreted over the years by the Supreme Court; they hold that if someone is being actively and lawfully arrested or if there is an immediate need to search and seize to prevent the destruction of evidence, the escape of a suspect, or imminent harm to someone, then warrants are usually not required by law. In this way, the Fourth Amendment is one of the many living and evolving facets of a complex legal framework designed to protect privacy and personal freedom from government overreach.

8. Based on the passage, which of the following actions would likely require a search warrant?
    a. Searching a suspect's vehicle during a routine traffic stop
    b. Searching a person's pockets during a lawful arrest
    c. Entering a private residence to prevent the destruction of evidence
    d. Searching a public area to ensure public safety

    The levels of force that police officers are authorized to use is one of many topics surrounding American law enforcement that regularly comes under heavy scrutiny. The Supreme Court has laid out various rulings that require clear justification when force is exerted by police officers. Several factors must be considered when determining what counts as reasonable use of force, key among which is the severity of the crime at hand; a more severe crime can be met with a proportionally more severe response. Other considerations include the severity of the threat posed to an officer or bystanders and the degree to which a suspect attempts to actively resist police orders. When someone resists arrest or tries to escape custody, officers may need to use more force than they would with someone who complies.

9. What is the primary consideration when evaluating the reasonableness of a law enforcement official's use of force?
    a. The severity of the crime that someone is suspected of committing
    b. The officer's history of enacting force
    c. The suspect's physical appearance or demographic characteristics
    d. The severity of the crime being actively committed by the suspect

> Qualified immunity functions as a shield for police officers and many other government officials. In essence, it protects officers from being held personally and monetarily liable for damages inflicted while in the line of duty, and it renders them immune from civil lawsuits for charges such as destruction of property. However, qualified immunity is not impenetrable and can be removed if an accusing plaintiff can prove that the officer in question infringed upon another person's constitutional rights during the incident in question. It is not enough to have caused harm or engaged in misconduct; the offense must have specifically infringed upon the constitutional rights of another person. In general, qualified immunity is designed as a safety net to protect officers from facing severe consequences for potential mistakes made in good faith while performing their duties. It also helps to shape the way that American citizens view and engage with law enforcement officers and government officials.

10. Based on the passage, under which circumstance would qualified immunity not apply?
    a. When demonstrated harm is caused to another person
    b. When misconduct by a police officer is provable
    c. When a public servant infringes on someone's constitutional rights
    d. When precedent exists from a similar incident

Written Expression

Directions: In the following sentences, choose the correct spelling of the missing word. Mark the letter that identifies your choice on the answer sheet.

1. Voting is a right for every American _____.
    a. siticin
    b. citizen
    c. citysen
    d. citisen

2. The _____ power outage accidentally tripped the alarm.
    a. momentery
    b. momenttary
    c. momentory
    d. momentary

3. It was his first day on the job, and he didn't want to make any _____.
    a. mistaks
    b. misstakes
    c. mistakes
    d. mitsakes

4. This was his first time getting to _____ such a serious crime.
    a. investigate
    b. invistagate
    c. envestigate
    d. investagate

5. Evidence in the case was brought quickly for _____ examination.
    a. ferensic
    b. forensic
    c. ferensec
    d. forensic

Directions: Read each sentence carefully and select the answer that is closest in meaning to the underlined word. Use prefix/suffix definitions and context clues to help eliminate incorrect answers.

6. The officer's testimony was required in court.
    a. Account
    b. Presence
    c. Litigation
    d. Attestation

7. Due to the isolated crime scene, witnesses were scarce.
    a. Angry
    b. Few
    c. Frightened
    d. Eager

8. The noisy house call spurred speculation.
    a. Restricted
    b. Expected
    c. Aroused
    d. Ignored

9. The detached witness turned out to be helpful.
    a. Inquisitive
    b. Cooperative
    c. Determined
    d. Disengaged

10. None of the onlookers doubted the driver's culpability.
    a. Innocence
    b. Fault
    c. Information
    d. Perspective

Reasoning

1. A man wakes up in the middle of the night to find that his home is being burglarized. The burglars, who are dressed all in black and wearing masks, flee as soon as the homeowner sees them. They get in a red sports car and take off. What would be the MOST useful piece of information that the man could give the police?
    a. A description of the car the burglars drove
    b. The approximate height and weight of each burglar
    c. The time the burglary happened
    d. The direction in which the burglars were driving

2. WITNESS STATEMENT: I was driving on Smith Street, and the guy behind me passed me and hit that guy on the motorbike in the other lane. I saw him behind me in my rear-view mirror. He was taking a drink of something; I don't know what it was.
Which event in the witness' statement happened first?
    a. The driver passed the witness.
    b. The witness started driving on Smith Street.
    c. The driver hit the guy on the motorbike.
    d. The driver took a drink of something.

3. A couple reports that their son has been missing since yesterday. What information from the parents will be MOST useful in locating their missing child?
    a. A physical description
    b. His name
    c. Where he was last seen
    d. Where his best friend lives

4. A woman reports that her purse was stolen. She says that she was leaving the bookstore on Main Street when a young man, possibly a teenager, ran up to her on her left side, grabbed her purse, continued running with the purse past her right side, and disappeared into the crowd. The woman claims that she didn't get a good look at the young man. Which event from the woman's statement happened first?
    a. A teenager grabbed her purse.
    b. A young man ran toward her left side.
    c. The thief disappeared into the crowd.
    d. The woman left the bookstore.

5. A man reports that his wife has been murdered. He claims that he came home from work to find her lying in a pool of blood on the kitchen floor. He says that his wife had been arguing with the neighbors recently. The neighbors in question are discovered to have been on vacation at the time of the murder, making the husband the prime suspect. What possible evidence could exonerate him as the murderer?
    a. The neighbors had a house sitter during their vacation.
    b. There is a suicide note on the kitchen counter.
    c. The man's workplace reports that he was at work at the time of death.
    d. The coroner finds that the woman had heroin in her system at the time of death.

Practice Test #3

6. Which of these cities is most different from the others?
    a. Rio de Janeiro
    b. New York City
    c. Chicago
    d. Denver

7. Which of the following words would be last, according to alphabetical order?
    a. Beautiful
    b. Bereavement
    c. Benefit
    d. Benevolent

8. If Jar A contains 55 marbles, and Jar B contains 42 marbles, how many marbles would remain in the two jars combined if a person removed five marbles from each jar?
    a. 97
    b. 92
    c. 87
    d. 77

9. In a race, Chris ran 100 meters in 10.21 seconds, Jim ran the distance in 10.67 seconds, Brian ran it in 10.50 seconds, and Trey finished the race in 10.36 seconds. Who won the race?
    a. Chris
    b. Jim
    c. Brian
    d. Trey

10. Which of the following body parts is different from the others?
    a. Kidney
    b. Liver
    c. Stomach
    d. Femur

11. Complete the sequence: triangle, square, pentagon, _____
    a. Circle
    b. Decathlon
    c. Octagon
    d. Hexagon

The next question is based upon the following graph:

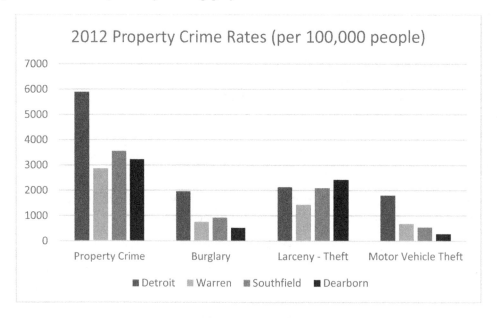

12. Which area had the lowest rates of property crime in 2012?
    a. Dearborn
    b. Detroit
    c. Southfield
    d. Warren

13. Which area had the greatest difference between larceny and burglary rates?
    a. Dearborn
    b. Detroit
    c. Southfield
    d. Warren

The next question is based upon the following table:

Percent Change in Offenses 2018-2019					
Township	Property crime	Burglary	Larceny-theft	Motor vehicle theft	Arson
Total	-3.1	-3.9	-7.3	-7.4	-0.3
Bethel	-2.6	-11.2	-0.3	-10.1	+0.2
Chartiers	-4.4	-11.5	-9.3	-12.7	-0.4
Fayette	-1.2	+2.1	-6.6	-4.6	-1.7
St. Clair	-5.0	-4.2	-9.9	-6.3	-3.4

14. In Fayette Township, which crime occurred more in 2019 than in 2018?
    a. Arson
    b. Burglary
    c. Larceny-theft
    d. Motor vehicle theft

15. OFFICER NOTES: July 4, 2019, around 2:15 a.m., arrived at 1518 Hawkins Blvd. in Kansas City, MO. Found paramedics treating a man, Ron Ortiz, outside the Tap Room bar. Mr. Ortiz and a witness, Diane Feliz, told me that a patron they didn't recognize hit Mr. Ortiz with a beer bottle while running past him after the bar closed. They gave a brief description of the person.
Which of the following options most clearly and accurately presents the facts from the report above?
    a. At 2:15 a.m. on July 4, 2019, I responded to a claim of assault at the Tap Room bar (1518 Hawkins Blvd). It's hard to tell if the victim, Ron Ortiz, was actually hit or if he was intoxicated and tripped, injuring himself. A witness named Diane Feliz did not offer much information.
    b. At 2:15 a.m. on July 4, 2019, I responded to a call at 1518 Hawkins Blvd. The victim, Ron Ortiz, suffered injuries after being hit with a beer bottle.
    c. I responded to the Tap Room bar at 2:15 a.m. on July 4, 2019, to investigate an injury. Ron Ortiz was struck with a beer bottle. I interviewed Ortiz and another witness. Her name was Diane Feliz. They did not recognize the person with the bottle.
    d. On July 4, 2019, at 2:15 a.m., I responded to the report of a suspected assault outside a bar at 1518 Hawkins Blvd. The victim, Ron Ortiz, was being treated for wounds on the back of his head. A witness, Diane Feliz, said she saw another man run past and strike Ortiz with a bottle. Though neither of them recognized the assailant, they were able to provide a description.

16. An officer responds to a violation of a noise ordinance at 3:00 a.m. When the officer arrives, very loud music is playing, and an occupant peers through the window. Before the occupant opens the door, the officer hears jostling and rustling inside. The occupant opens the door and apologizes for the music. When the officer peers inside the home through the open door, he sees a digital scale and small plastic bags on the table. The home also has a suspicious odor.
Which of the following conclusions can be made from the statement above?
    a. The noises inside the home indicate a dispute or assault.
    b. The officer was called to the wrong home; there were no violations of the law.
    c. There is no indication of any crime beyond the noise ordinance violation.
    d. There is probable cause to enter the home under suspicion of drug possession.

17. WITNESS STATEMENT: The attacker had some type of a metal rod. It looked like a baton from a race. He hit the victim in the face and knocked him down, then he hit him with the baton about five or six more times before running away. The attacker was about my height, 5'8", and was a heavy-set White guy with a beard. Probably about thirty years old.
Which of the given details would be MOST important in finding the suspect?
    a. His physical description
    b. His age
    c. His choice of weapon
    d. The number of times he struck the victim

18. Place the following statements in order so that they follow a logical sequence: 1) The burglar dropped the TV on the floor, waking the owner. 2) The burglar escaped out of the bedroom window. 3) The burglar grabbed the small TV in the bedroom. 4) The burglar climbed into the bedroom window.
    a. 1, 2, 3, 4
    b. 4, 3, 2, 1
    c. 4, 3, 1, 2
    d. 1, 3, 2, 4

19. Complete the sequence: ZXY...WUV...TRS...?
    a. QOP
    b. QPO
    c. OPQ
    d. OQP

20. Steve drove 20 minutes from his home to Mary's house to pick her up for a date. They had been together for four hours when Steve dropped Mary off at her house. Steve then drove home and parked his car in the driveway at 11:35 p.m. At what time did Steve leave home to pick up Mary?
    a. 6:25 p.m.
    b. 6:35 p.m.
    c. 6:45 p.m.
    d. 6:55 p.m.

Answer Explanations #3

Memorization

1. C: There are 9 laptops in the image.

2. B: There are 8 people standing in the image.

3. C: There are 2 drinking water dispensers in the image.

4. A: In the graph in the background, all of the results are showing an increase.

5. D: There are 6 plants in the entire office building.

6. B: There is a man selling popcorn at the park.

7. D: A girl is hanging upside down in the park.

8. B: There is a swing set in the picture.

9. C: There are 4 buckets of popcorn on the counter of the popcorn stand.

10. C: 5 people are sitting down in the picture.

Written Comprehension

1. C: This answer best identifies the main idea of the passage, which is to detail the requirements of becoming a K-9 officer. Police dogs do typically live and work with their handlers, and this is a long-term commitment, but these answers represent supporting details of the passage, not the main idea. Patrol experience is typically a requirement of becoming a K-9 officer, but again this is a supporting detail, not the main idea of the passage.

2. A: Based on the passage, this statement best defines the term *disability*, which is a physical or mental impairment that limits a person in at least one major aspect of life. While visual, speech, and hearing impairments can be considered disabilities, they are examples of a disability and not a comprehensive definition. Illnesses such as the flu are temporary and cannot be considered a disability, nor is this a definition for the term *disability*. While these mental illnesses may be considered disabilities, again they are examples and not a comprehensive definition of the term *disability*.

3. D: Choice *D* is correct because the passage connects a strong bond of community trust with the willingness of residents to aid and support local law enforcement. Choices *A*, *B*, and *C* are incorrect because all incorrectly define the aim of community trust.

4. D: Choice *D* is correct because the passage highlights that social media enables better communication between police officers and their communities, thereby building trust. Choice *A* is incorrect because the passage specifically mentions that online visibility is a threat to the safety of officers. Choice *B* is incorrect because the passage makes no mention of using social media to track criminals. Choice *C* is incorrect because the passage specifically discusses that the spread of misinformation is a threat, not a benefit.

5. C: Choice C is correct because the exclusionary rule bans illegally acquired evidence from legal consideration, thus discouraging officers from overstepping their boundaries to acquire evidence. Choice A is incorrect because the exclusionary rule does not affect a person's rights. Choices B and D are incorrect because the rule exists specifically to discount illegal evidence.

6. A: Choice A is correct because search warrants are given out primarily based on probable cause. Choices B and D have nothing to do with probable cause and are not mentioned in the passage. Choice C is incorrect because arrest warrants inform people of their rights while in custody, making them more about providing information than about granting legal permissions.

7. A: Choice A is correct because, according to the passage, when police use their discretion unlawfully or unethically, they can make decisions that harm citizens' views of law enforcement. Choice B is incorrect because the passage claims that the flexibility of police discretion increases efficiency. Choice C is incorrect because public trust is threatened by the abuse of authority, not the presence of it. Choice D is incorrect because the passage clearly states that discretion helps officers in the management of resource allocation.

8. A: Choice A is correct because a person's vehicle is their private property, which means that the Fourth Amendment applies in this scenario. Choice B is incorrect because the passage states that the Fourth Amendment does not apply to those undergoing lawful arrest. Choice C is incorrect because preventing the destruction of evidence is an exception that does not require a warrant. Choice D is incorrect because the Fourth Amendment exclusively concerns private areas and private property.

9. D: Choice D is correct because the text mentions that the severity of the crime being committed is the most important factor to consider when evaluating whether the use of force was justified. Choice A is incorrect because the use of force is less likely to be necessary when a crime is not being actively committed. Choices B and C are irrelevant factors when evaluating the justification of police force.

10. C: Choice C is correct because qualified immunity applies unless an officer demonstrably infringed upon someone's constitutional rights during the occurrence in question. Choices A and B are incorrect because personal harm or misconduct alone does not negate qualified immunity. Choice D is incorrect because precedent does not appear to have any bearing on qualified immunity, according to the passage.

Written Expression

1. B: citizen

2. D: momentary

3. C: mistakes

4. A: investigate

5. B: forensic

6. D: *Testimony* is used in this context as a noun that refers to one's sworn account. Whereas *account* captures one part of the word's meaning, *attestation* captures both parts, as it is a sworn account. Both *presence* and *litigation* do not fit in this context.

Answer Explanations #3

7. B: While each of the choices fit in the sentence as adjectives used to describe the witnesses, only *few* matches the meaning of *scarce*. Both words describe the quantity of the witnesses, while *angry*, *frightened*, and *eager* describe the state of being of the witnesses, so they are irrelevant to the context.

8. C: *Spurred* is used in this sentence to describe the effect of the noisy house call. Whereas *restricted* indicates an effect, it does not match the definition of the word in context. *Aroused* is the only choice that indicates the same effect of the house call as the word in question. Neither *expected* nor *ignored* fit the sentence.

9. D: *Detached* is used as an adjective in this sentence to describe the actions, presentation, or behavior of the witness. Both *inquisitive* and *cooperative* have opposite meanings of the word in the sentence. *Determined* also misses the mark because it implies that the witness was an active participant in the events. The definition of *disengaged*—to show little interest or awareness—matches the word in the sentence.

10. B: *Culpability* is used as a noun in this sentence, and the apostrophe and *s* at the end of *driver's* indicates that the *culpability* is possessed by the driver. Therefore, all of the answer choices could fit in the sentence because they are all nouns. *Fault* is the only answer choice that matches the definition of the word in question, however. Neither *innocence*, *information*, nor *perspective* match the definition of the word in question.

Reasoning

1. A: Choice *A* is correct because a description of the getaway car is probably the most useful piece of information, as it could help narrow down the field of suspects tremendously if enough details are given. Choice *B* is incorrect because an approximate height and weight may not be accurate. Even if they are, lots of people might fit the measurements without any additional information, such as hair color, complexion, etc. Choice *C* is incorrect because the time of the burglary would give very little information about the suspects, other than the fact that they were awake at an unusual time. Choice *D* is incorrect because the burglars could have changed their direction on the road at any time.

2. B: Choice *B* is correct because the witness started driving on Smith Street before the rest of the events occurred. Choices *A*, *C*, and *D* are incorrect because they all occurred on Smith Street, after the witness had begun to drive on it.

3. A: Choice *A* is correct because a physical description of the child will be most useful in the search. Choice *B* is incorrect because the boy might not be within listening distance and it is easier and faster to identify someone based on appearance. Choice *C* is incorrect because the boy might be far away from where he was last seen if it was a day ago. Choice *D* is incorrect because the likelihood that the boy is with his friend or that his friend knows his whereabouts is minimal.

4. D: Choice *D* is correct because the woman leaving the bookstore was the first event from the statement that she reported. Choices *A*, *B*, and *C* are incorrect because they occurred after she left the bookstore. Additionally, Choice *A* is also incorrect because the woman wasn't sure if it was a teenager or a young man that grabbed her purse.

5. C: Choice *C* is correct because if the man's workplace can confirm that he was at work at the time of death, then it would not be possible for him to have killed his wife. Choice *A* is incorrect because the neighbors having a house sitter does not provide an alibi for the husband; it only adds a person to

Answer Explanations #3

question. Choice *B* is incorrect because it is possible that the husband wrote the note before or after killing his wife, although this is inconsistent with reporting that his wife was murdered. Choice *D* is incorrect because the wife still could have been murdered by her husband, even if she had drugs in her system.

6. A: Choice *A* is correct because, of the four cities, Rio do Janeiro is the only one that is not in the United States. Choices *B*, *C*, and *D* are incorrect because they are all cities in the United States.

7. B: Choice *B* is correct because when the words are put in alphabetical order, the word *bereavement* is last. Although all the words start with *b* followed by *e*, Choice *A* is incorrect because "bea-" comes before "ber-." Choices *C* and *D* are incorrect because "ben-" comes before "ber-" as well.

8. C: Choice *C* is correct for the following reason: The two jars originally contained 97 marbles when combined (55 + 42 = 97). By removing five marbles from each jar, a person would remove 10 total marbles, leaving a combined total of 87 marbles. Choice *A* is incorrect because that is the original number of marbles. Choice *B* is incorrect because that would be the remaining number of marbles if five were removed from only one jar. Choice *D* is incorrect because that would be the remaining number of marbles if 10 were removed from each jar.

9. A: Choice *A* is correct because Chris ran the distance in less time (10.21 seconds) than Jim (10.67 seconds), Brian (10.50 seconds), and Trey (10.36 seconds). As a result, Choices *B*, *C*, and *D* are incorrect.

10. D: Choice *D* is correct because the femur is a bone and all the other choices are soft organs. Additionally, the femur is part of the leg, while the others are all located in the torso.

11. D: Choice *D* is correct because the sequence is a series of shapes, with each shape in the list having one more side than previously listed shape. A triangle has three sides, a square has four sides, a pentagon has five sides, and the next shape in the sequence is a hexagon, which has six sides. Choice *A* is incorrect because a circle has an infinite number of sides, Choice *B* is incorrect because a decathlon is an Olympic event, not a shape. Choice *C* is incorrect because an octagon has 8 sides.

12. D: On the graph, the lightest gray bar represents Warren. For the data labeled "Property Crime" on the graph, that bar is the smallest, meaning the rates of property crime were lowest in that area. Choices *A*, *B*, and *C* are incorrect because the bars representing Dearborn, Detroit, and Southfield for the data labeled "Property Crime" on the graph are all taller than the bar for Warren, meaning they all had higher rates of property crime.

13. A: The difference between the Dearborn (darkest gray) bars for larceny and burglary is about 1,900, which is the greatest difference for any of the areas. Choice *B* is incorrect because the difference between the Detroit bars for larceny and burglary is about 170, which is less than 1,900. Choice *C* is incorrect because the difference between the Southfield bars for larceny and burglary is about 1,200, which is less than 1,900. Choice *D* is incorrect because the difference between the Warren bars for larceny and burglary is about 690, which is less than 1,900.

14. B: Burglary in Fayette Township changed by +2.1%, which is a 2.1% increase, the largest increase of any crime listed in that township. Choice *A* is incorrect because arson decreased by 1.7% in Fayette Township. Choice *C* is incorrect because larceny-theft decreased by 6.6% in Fayette Township. Choice *D* is incorrect because motor vehicle theft decreased by 6.3% in Fayette Township.

15. D: This choice presents the most relevant information from the notes in the most logical order. Choice *A* includes unnecessary opinions while also omitting useful details. Choice *B* omits helpful details. Choice *C* omits details and is not organized as clearly.

16. D: The plastic bags, scale, and odor all suggest the presence of drugs, while the rustling before opening the door suggests the resident was hiding something before opening the door. Choice *A* is incorrect because there are no signs of a dispute or assault. Choice *B* is incorrect because the music was playing very loudly when the officer arrived at the house for the noise ordinance call. Choice *C* is incorrect because there is indication of the presence of drugs in the home.

17. A: Choice *A* is correct because the suspect's physical description is the most important information in the witness' statement. Choice *B* is incorrect because the suspect's exact age is not known; the estimated age only adds to the physical description. Choice *C* is incorrect because the weapon could easily be discarded. Choice *D* is incorrect because the number of times he struck the victim tells nothing about the suspect that would help in locating him.

18. C: Choice *C* is correct because the burglar climbed into the bedroom window, grabbed the TV, dropped it, and then escaped through the bedroom window. Choices *A* and *D* are incorrect because they would indicate that the burglar escaped through the bedroom window before climbing into the bedroom, which isn't possible. Choice *B* is incorrect because it indicates that the burglar dropped the TV on the floor after escaping through the window, which also isn't possible.

19. A: Choice *A* is correct because this sequence is defined by working backward through the alphabet in three-letter chunks. However, the letters within each chunk are jumbled such that the last letter becomes the first of the chunk, followed by the first letter, and then the second letter. The three letters before RST are OPQ; putting these letters in the correct order for the sequence creates QOP, Choice *A*. Choices *B*, *C*, and *D* are incorrect because, while they use the correct letters, they are not in the correct order.

20. D: Choice *D* is correct because Steve's total time away from home was 4 hours and 40 minutes: 4 hours for the date and 40 minutes for travel to and from Mary's house. Turning back the clock from 11:35 p.m. by 4 hours and 40 minutes means that Steve left his house at 6:55 p.m. Choices *A*, *B*, and *C* are incorrect because they make Steve's time away from home greater than 4 hours and 40 minutes.

Dear CJBAT Test Taker,

Thank you for purchasing this study guide for your CJBAT exam. We hope that we exceeded your expectations.

Our goal in creating this study guide was to cover all of the topics that you will see on the test. We also strove to make our practice questions as similar as possible to what you will encounter on test day. With that being said, if you found something that you feel was not up to your standards, please send us an email and let us know.

We would also like to let you know about another book in our catalog that may interest you.

Civil Service Exam

amazon.com/dp/1637758561

We have study guides in a wide variety of fields. If the one you are looking for isn't listed above, then try searching for it on Amazon or send us an email.

Thanks Again and Happy Testing!
Product Development Team
info@studyguideteam.com

Online Resources & Audiobook Access

Included with your purchase are multiple online resources. This includes all three practice tests in interactive format and this study guide in audiobook format. We also have a convenient study timer to help you manage your time.

Scan the QR code or go to this link to access this content:

testprepbooks.com/online387/cjbat

The first time you access the tests, you will need to register as a "new user" and verify your email address.

If you have any issues, please email support@testprepbooks.com.

Made in United States
Orlando, FL
27 June 2025